MATT KLEINMAN

SHOW ME THE MON£Y!

An insider's guide to becoming a top level professional footballer

All rights reserved. No part of this publication may be reproduced, stored in or introduced into a retrieval system, or transmitted, in any form, or by any means (electronic, mechanical, photocopying, recording or otherwise) without the prior written permission of the publisher.

This book is sold subject to the condition that it shall not, by way of trade or otherwise, be lent, re-sold, hired out, or otherwise circulated without the publisher's prior consent in any form of binding or cover other than that in which it is published and without a similar condition including this condition being imposed on the subsequent purchaser.

DISCLAIMER

Please note that the comments made by the author are based on the rules and regulations in place at the time of writing. However, these are subject to change and may not remain the author's views when new rule changes are implemented.

ACKNOWLEDGEMENTS

As with any long season that endures the highs and lows of victory and defeat, bitter cold weather mixed with warmth and sunshine, bad luck versus good fortune, success ultimately results in a team effort. Writing this book and bringing it to its final form was no different in so much as, it would not have been possible without the support and encouragement of some key individuals.

I extend a huge amount of gratitude to Huw Jennings for writing the foreword. I don't believe that there is anyone else in youth football in the UK better placed to contribute. Huw is responsible for having brought through the likes of Theo Walcott, Nathan Dyer, Gareth Bale, Adam Lallana, Matt Mills, Dexter Blackstock, Alex Oxlade-Chamberlain and Leon Best (to name just a few) at Southampton. He also worked as a Youth Development Manager at the FA Premier League before taking up his current role as the Youth Academy Director at Fulham.

Steve Beaglehole, Des Bulpin, Peter Horne, Julian Rhodes, Steve Quashie, Solomon Abrahams, David Burke and Ross Wilson were fantastic in sharing their wealth of experience and expertise in youth football.

An extra special mention goes to Don Graham who worked tirelessly to support me and whose contribution towards creating the end product deserves his name attached to it as much as mine.

Thanks also to Keith Koster for his knowledge and advice on publishing.

Finally, a heartfelt gratitude to the best football agent in the industry, who I'm privileged to call my business partner and even more so, my close friend – Alex Levack. I thank him for his passion, support and unwavering belief in our shared vision.

ABOUT THE AUTHOR

Matt Kleinman is an English FA Licensed Football Agent with 14 years of experience in the industry. In that time he has represented players at international level, at all levels in the professional game in England and brokered several international transfers into territories such as Europe, Southern Africa, Australasia and the US.

Matt has always been a passionate supporter and, indeed, regular player of 'the beautiful game'. In 1998, after graduating from Birmingham University with a BA honours degree in Sport and Leisure Management, he landed a role with a boutique Law Firm that represented some of the leading European-based South African footballers.

Matt subsequently worked alongside the well known Sports Lawyer, Mel Stein - most famous for having represented the likes of Chris Waddle, Paul Gascoigne and Alan Shearer - and with one of the top global football agencies at that time, First Artist Plc.

The likes of Lucas Radebe, Mark Fish, Shaun Bartlett, Neil Lennon, Michael Turner, Jermaine Beckford, Alexander Hleb, Ashley Young, Adam Lallana and Micah Richards are just a few of the players that Matt has been involved with over the years.

During his time in the game, Matt has witnessed at first-hand the many challenges that face a young man who wishes to become a top professional player. He has seen both those who have reached the higher echelons of the game and those that showed potential but sadly failed to live up to it. A strong and supportive presence in the lives of the players that he represents, Matt has become a master at guiding young footballers into the first category.

This book is a culmination of Matt's vast experience of the highs and lows of looking after a young footballer aiming for the dizzy heights of Premier League and even international football. It is this knowledge and first-class ability to deliver for his clients that has drawn many top players to him at Sidekick Management.

It's the team that drives the dream!

For further information about the company visit the website: www.sidekickmanagement.co.uk.

FORWARD
By Huw Jennings of Fulham FC

Most of us have very sophisticated methods of navigation to help us find where we are going. Interactive maps, sat navs and GPS are just some of the tools that we utilise. Now, barely any location is exempt from our gaze. Typically, we zoom in on our proposed holiday location to determine how far it is away from the beach. If you are looking for somewhere new to live, it's virtually possible to examine the type of curtains in the property from your home computer. We look very carefully at where we want to go and how to get there.

You would think that the same level of scrutiny would be applied to pursuing a career in professional football. At face value it is. We have dedicated 24:7 television channels to inform us and are swamped by no end of alternative media. There is no doubt that the pathway that the game follows has never been more closely examined. However, in my experience this does not apply to the early stages of the journey. Yes, families will rightly hold clubs to account for education provision and they will want feedback from the club's coaches. But they are often wary of asking too many questions for fear of getting an unfavourable reputation. Worse still, they may get sucked in by touchline gossip and start believing that the opinion of the most vociferous parent is accurate. Even more alarmingly, some parents become susceptible to the banter of characters who hang around young players purporting to be agents.

With this in mind, it is worth reflecting on how parents normally operate when gaining information on activities for their children. It would be unheard of for, let's say, the parent of a talented swimmer to believe that the advice they receive from a guy who has watched their child's session from the balcony of a leisure complex to be more authoritative than that of the coach. Why some parents elect to take this type of advice in a comparable football context is baffling.

Unquestionably, what has been lacking as support material for the journey is an authentic manual written in straight forward language by someone who has good experience and high moral standards. Step forward Matt Kleinman and, 'Show Me The Mon£y!'. Here is a book that tells you as it is and gives the reader the information that they require.

I have had lots of dealings with Matt over the years although funnily enough we have never done a deal on a player. He is conscientious and ethical in his approach and this guide comes from someone who cares about the person as well as the player.

I have always believed that young players and their families are entitled to independent advice and as such have never had a difficulty in working alongside agents who have the right qualities. Matt possesses these in abundance and this book provides the ideal starting point for the right independent advice to help you navigate correctly along the windy road that is professional football.

Good luck!

CONTENTS

Introduction

Chapter 1　Finding An Agent　　　　　　　　　　　　　　1

    When to start looking for an agent　　　　　　　　　　1
    Agents from a club's perspective　　　　　　　　　　　3
    Selecting an agent　　　　　　　　　　　　　　　　　5
    Trust and respect　　　　　　　　　　　　　　　　　6
    Complete transparency　　　　　　　　　　　　　　　8
    Communication is key　　　　　　　　　　　　　　　9
    Take your time　　　　　　　　　　　　　　　　　　10
    Be loyal　　　　　　　　　　　　　　　　　　　　　12
    What if you choose badly and you wish to get out of the agent representation agreement?　　　　　　　　　　　13

Chapter 2　Representation Agreements　　　　　　　　　15

    How the agent gets paid　　　　　　　　　　　　　　15
    How and when commissions are paid to the agent　　16
    Unscrupulous agents　　　　　　　　　　　　　　　17
    Who can act as an agent?　　　　　　　　　　　　　17
    The PFA　　　　　　　　　　　　　　　　　　　　　19
    What a player/agent representation agreement looks like　20
    Commercial contracts　　　　　　　　　　　　　　　27

Chapter 3　Sholarships　　　　　　　　　　　　　　　　29

    Travelling time/distance becomes redundant　　　　30
    The scholarship process　　　　　　　　　　　　　　30
    When is a scholarship contract offered to a player?　33
    When a player can trial at another club　　　　　　33
    Beware of the vultures　　　　　　　　　　　　　　34
    Inducements are illegal　　　　　　　　　　　　　　35
    Dealing with being released by a club　　　　　　　35
    A club's perspective on releasing players　　　　　36
    The agent's role when a player is released by a club　38

Chapter 4 Moving Clubs – Time For A Fresh Start	41
Taking one step back to take three steps forward	41
Biggest isn't always best!	42
Reserve team scrapped	43
Getting out on loan	45
Compensation – a scary word	46
When compensation is payable	48
Elite Player Performance Plan (EPPP)	49
How will the new system affect young players?	50

Chapter 5 Goal Setting	59
Setting clearly defined goals	59
Goals are the roadmap to success	60
So you want to be a player then, do you?	60
What do you want to achieve in your playing career?	61
Don't just work hard, work harder than others	62
Reputation is key	63
What do you want to achieve in your personal life?	64
A friend in need is a friend indeed - committing to achieving your goals	65
We are the products of our thoughts	66
Vision boards	66

Chapter 6 Achieving Goals Through Selecting Good Mentors	69
Copy someone who's achieved what you want to achieve in the football world	69
Find someone at your club from whom to seek inspiration	70
Read!!!	71
Mentors outside of football	71
Try not to burn your bridges	72

Chapter 7	Work Hard On Yourself	75
	Personal development	75
	Mental/psychological development	76
	Take your training seriously	77
	Eat well	78
	Consider doing pilates and yoga to improve your core strength and flexibility and stave off injuries	79
	Don't take your education for granted	80
	Manage your income and expenditure	82
	Time management	83
	Discipline is key	83

Chapter 8	Praise And Support	87
	A good agent earns his stripes	87
	Having an inflated opinion of your son's ability	88
	Pushy parents are a recipe for disaster	89
	Approaching coaches and managers	90
	A good agent makes themselves redundant	90
	The 3 R's for building rapport – Respect, Respect, Respect	92
	Positivity	93
	Supportive parents	95
	Building rapport with agents	96
	Negativity is all around us	98

Appendix	Standard Football Association Representation Agreement between a licensed agent and a player	103

INTRODUCTION

"Before the Premier League came into being, youngsters just had to be the best in their region in order to be signed on. Now they have to be among the best in the world because the demands are so much higher. There is much more competition and it is harder than ever for youngsters to make it, but that has led to an overall improvement in standards, which has to be good for the national game."

Mike Foster, General Secretary of The Barclays Premier League. Article on the Premier League website, 17th November 2011

As the pressure mounts on teenagers to 'make it' in the increasingly competitive world of professional football, this book sets out to serve as a guide for parents and young players.

Over the course of the book, I will address such issues as:
- When and how to speak to coaches and managers
- The mindset and attitude required to break through in today's professional game and establish a long and successful career
- The pros and cons of having an agent
- How to find a good one

Crucially, I will also look at which circumstances may require you actually to hire an agent (including what should and should not be contained within a representation agreement). There is also a section on scholarships that seeks to provide the reader with a clearer insight into the rights of the player before and after being offered a contract by his club.

It is my aim to enable a clearer understanding of the football industry, by giving you a comprehensive view of the business through the eyes of an agent. The knowledge I will share with you in this book is based on the numerous successes, failures and rule changes I have seen in my work since 1998.

I have also interviewed a number of highly experienced club officials for this book, from coaches and managers to heads of recruitment, directors and chairmen, gauging clubs' perspectives as well as my own. The aim is to 'thin-slice' the industry for you, and reveal its many different layers.

Should you have any further questions, please feel free to get in touch with me. You can contact me through my company, Sidekick Management at info@sidekickmanagement.com.

Matt Kleinman

CHAPTER 1
FINDING THE RIGHT AGENT

> **❝** I will not rest until I have you holding a Coke, wearing your own shoe, playing a Sega game featuring you, while singing your own song in a new commercial, starring you, broadcast during the Superbowl, in a game that you are winning, and I will not **sleep** until that happens. I'll give you fifteen minutes to call me back. **❞**
>
> Jerry Maguire in the movie, Jerry Maguire 1996

When to start looking for an agent

There is a real mixture of opinions regarding when a player first needs the services of a licensed agent. Some argue that it is not necessary until after the player's first professional contract is signed. In fact, there was one Premier League club in the mid-2000s that pretty much banned its youth players from having any representation in the form of a licensed agent, a controversial stance that wasn't strictly legal. Every footballer over the age of sixteen is legally entitled to representation.

I can understand that club's viewpoint, if they were seeking to have every single player on exactly the same terms, salary and contract duration. If that was the goal, the club would argue that there is no scope for negotiation: take it or leave it!

But it's usually not quite as simple as that.

Some players hold a greater value to a club than others. For example, Wayne

Rooney would not have been offered the same terms for his first professional contract as other 17-year-old players at Everton at the time. If he had been, it is almost certain that the likes of Manchester United, Liverpool and the other top English teams would have intervened, offering him considerably more money to sign for them. This is the problem that clubs are faced with when trying to balance what's right for the club and what's right for the player.

So how could increased wages be bad for a player? It's not as simple a question as it seems. A large salary coupled with lots of free time can create a scenario that is detrimental to a young player's development. Quite rightly, clubs want their young players to focus on their football education and progression as players, rather than adopting the "I've already made it" mentality; and premature riches can moderate a young player's hunger to achieve his potential. How does somebody who has never had to deal with financial success stop themselves from becoming more complacent when they achieve it, less motivated to improve?

There is also the worry from the club's perspective that a difference in wages (especially a large one) between players at, say, 17 or 18 years of age will breed jealousy. There is often a perception on the part of the lesser-paid player that the club does not value him as greatly as his team-mate. For this reason alone, many clubs try extremely hard to offer exactly the same financial package to all players on their first professional contract.

Even though football is a very subjective business, I have found that players often look at their contemporaries and make direct comparisons. They question whether their team-mate or opponent is better, and quite often conclude that they aren't. This, in turn, begs the question: "why should player X be receiving higher pay than me?!" While I can appreciate this argument, my advice is usually the same to young players: focus on yourself and nobody else (unless you have a mentor that you can model and help to improve your game). Never focus on the money – in the long term you will make up the financial difference. In the short term, big financial goals will keep you away from achieving your main target – to be the best player you can possibly be.

The distraction of finance is just that: an unnecessary distraction.

If anything, your son should use the desire for greater pay as motivation to work harder, and improve faster, so that an increase in wages can be better justified. It is my belief that the moment money becomes his number one driving factor, a young footballer loses sight of why he started a career in the first place: a genuine love of playing the game, the feeling of winning, and the sense of accomplishment that comes with being part of a successful team.

In other words, don't chase the money. Let the money chase you!

Agents from a club's perspective

The general consensus among football clubs is that agents play a necessary role in the game. While many clubs would suggest that agents can be a poisonous influence on players – unsettling them in order to push through transfers and make themselves money – in reality, as in any industry, there are some good guys and some bad guys. As Steve Beaglehole at Leicester City says,

"You've got to move with the times. The best 16-18 year olds in the UK have agents. In fact, I would suggest that the majority of players, not just the best, in those age ranges have an agent – and you won't change that.

The way I look at it is this – we are constantly being told that coaches are stifling players' development and coaching natural ability out of them. This is absolutely true if you have a bad coach. That is the same with agents. You get good and bad agents too.

I'm not a big lover of the term 'agent,' as I think it throws up all sorts of negative connotations. I prefer the term 'manager,' as that is what many of these people do – they help manage and mentor young players."

Across industries, the agent, the 'middle man,' has a notorious reputation. Take estate agents for example: the mere mention of the term 'estate agent' conjures up an image in many peoples' minds of a middle man looking only to earn their commission, with little genuine interest in taking care of the client's needs. The words 'greedy' 'unscrupulous' and 'immoral' are often bandied about when elaborating this image! But stereotypes are easy to make: again, there are good estate agents and there are not-so-good ones. It is wrong to tarnish everyone with the same brush.

This assessment seems to be widely supported by clubs. For example, Ross Wilson, Head of football business at Watford FC, suggests:

"Agents have got a bad name. Undoubtedly there are some operating who are very poor, but they are in the minority. I believe that agents have earned a place in the game. The best agents offer the best career advice rather than just being all about money. This is especially the case where young players are concerned. The best agents recognise this and help players make the right choices for the short, medium and long-term."

David Burke, Head of Football Operations at Brighton & Hove Albion, also believes that agents are now a key part of the football business; but his thoughts on the relationship between young players and their agents are slightly different from those of Steve Beaglehole and Ross Wilson:

> "It is an uncontrollable part of the game which clubs cannot affect. Therefore, one needs to be open minded and communicative with agents, as it's a three-way relationship."

One point at which a football agent certainly does play a valuable role is when they come to negotiating their client's contract. Here, the agent acts as a buffer between the club and the player, making the negotiation a less 'personal' reflection of that player. The player has to face the club and its management every day; the agent does not.

I have seen plenty of examples where a player has sought to negotiate his own deal with the club, and has gone in with a wage demand that the club is unwilling to meet. Not only can this sort of disagreement breed ill feeling, but it can also create ammunition to be used against the player in training and matches, invariably rearing its head when the player has a poor training session or match.

Clearly, in cases like this, the club is in a far stronger position in the contract negotiation process than the player, and in such instances the presence of an agent can often be deemed a bit of a nuisance by the club; conversely, though, clubs tend to recognise that agents provide a valuable source of general support to players, taking on the burden of duties that might otherwise become the responsibility of the club, with positive implications for the club's time and manpower. Examples of this might include helping a player source a car, sorting out insurance, arranging mortgage for a new home, and so on.

Julian Rhodes, the Chairman at Bradford City, who has experienced the emotional highs of Premier League Football contrasted with a series of relegations through to League 2 also supports the claim that players need agents, especially during the contract negotiation process. He also echoes Ross Wilson's sentiments about there being good ones as well as bad ones in the industry and the additional benefit of agents dealing with off-pitch affairs for players so that they can focus fully on their duties on it.

> "Every player should have an agent when they are a professional and doing a contract negotiation. It's a competitive marketplace and the player needs to get the best deal he can for himself. However, I do believe that players should be the ones paying the agent and not the club. I'm not sure at what age it should happen. I'm not bothered when a player has an agent, I'm sick of people

whinging about agents. There are good ones and bad ones. A player needs to be focused purely on playing football and he needs an agent to do that."

Selecting an agent

It can be confusing being approached by numerous agents, all promising the world to your son. You'll hear all sorts of things. Here are some examples of the type of 'spiel' you might get:

"I have great contacts at all levels..."

"There isn't a door that I can't open!"

"I know the manager personally. I have a great relationship with him."

"In the representation contract it says that I'll charge you x per cent, but I assure you that you'll never have to pay me a penny. I'll get my commission from the club."

The player usually signs a standard two-year representation contract with the agent whose overtures have impressed the most; but in many cases, before the playing contract that the agent negotiates for him has expired, the player will end up severing ties with that agent. He'll move elsewhere – invariably to join up with a so-called 'bigger player' in the industry who promises to deliver better results.

While it is clearly important to select an agent with good connections with clubs (that is to say, with managers, chairmen, directors and coaches), in my opinion it is far more important that the agent you select is trustworthy and hard-working.

Remember, though: an agent can open doors, but he can't put his player's boots on and go out and perform for him in training and matches. In actuality, a player's destiny is in his own hands: if he is good enough, has the correct attitude, and is prepared to work, he will get to the level that he should be playing at; with or without the help of any agent.

My advice to young players and their parents is to ask other players who their agent is, and find out what those agents do for them. Ask if their agent comes to watch their games, speaks with them regularly, maintains a good relationship with them.

Most importantly, ask if the agent has been there for the player through tough times as well as good ones. After all, it's easy for an agent to look after an outstanding young player when he's performing fantastically and lots of clubs, sponsors, and sportswear manufacturers are chasing him down for a piece of the action. However, my belief is that a good agent – and, for that matter, a good person – shows their true colours in times of adversity: when the player is not getting into the team, when his form has dipped, when he's going through tough times with his girlfriend or family, or perhaps when he's suffering from an injury that is getting him down. During these times, an agent shows his true worth. The agent that has the integrity, the agent who will 'walk the talk' delivered at the start of his relationship with his player, will simply show up. He'll be there to provide the support, care and skill that his young charge desperately requires.

In order for your son to overcome the more challenging times (and there will be plenty ahead), it is critical that he has a great support network around him of people who care for him, and whom he can trust one hundred per cent. A player's journey from scholar to professional to established, well-paid pro is rarely a smooth one. More often than not, it is a full-on rollercoaster ride, with great highs and painful lows. In modern football there are very few players who have emerged from youth teams, secured professional contracts, progressed through reserve teams, broken into first teams and continued to hold down a place in the same sides for the remainder of their career. The likes of Gary Neville, Paul Scholes, Ryan Giggs, Jamie Carragher and Steven Gerrard are the captive pandas (in a good way) of the football world – a real rarity!

My tip for your son is this: always stay close to the friends he knew before he was successful, and always listen to people he knows have his best interests at heart.

Trust and respect

As is the case with any relationship, trust and respect between a player and agent has to be earned over a period of time. A good agent will be there to deal with some of the most private issues in your son's life – not only his finances, but also his personal problems, should he wish to confide. This is a common scenario that comes with the one-to-one nature of the player/agent relationship.

I would strongly question the motives of an agent who pushes your son into a decision, or forces him to sign anything. I believe an agent should be there to provide the player with options, not to make choices on his behalf. By all means, the agent should explain to the player and his guardian(s) what the pros and cons are of each scenario, but ultimately the player must be allowed to decide what works best for him. This is for two reasons: firstly, an agent should never be accused of bullying a player into doing something that he doesn't want to do; secondly, the player must learn to take responsibility for his own choices in life. Only in this way is he truly the master of his own destiny.

When signing a Representation Agreement with an agent, I would always encourage you to check that a clause is inserted that allows the player and his guardian to seek legal advice on the contract. This clause must be in the agreement, or the agreement is not congruent with FA regulations. I would also always advise having the contract checked by a solicitor. You may find something within it that is prohibitive or unfair – and if you do, it wouldn't seem to me to be the best start to what is supposed to be a trusting relationship. Unless a genuine error has occurred, I would encourage you to ask yourself: "is this the sort of person that I want my son to sign for?"

Choose carefully, and don't let yourself be rushed by anyone. I have known of large companies turning up to meetings accompanied by established first team players and internationals that they represent in order to influence a youngster to sign with them. It can be hard to reject overtures from agents that represent big name players when they argue that they have delivered outstanding results for those clients. But while in most cases the kudos are justified, the question you must ask is whether you feel they will focus as much attention on your lad when times aren't quite so glorious.

I represent a player (let's call him 'Luke') who originally signed with one of the larger agencies. At the age of 16, Luke was mooted as a future first team Premier League player, and possibly a full England international. Unfortunately for him, however, such glory has not since materialised. When the original agent came to pitch their services to Luke and his family, he turned up with an England international in tow: inevitably, Luke signed for that company, in good faith, and with understandable optimism for his future. After all, it was now in such 'esteemed' hands.

Sadly, today Luke tells me about how, during a later, more difficult phase of his career, things changed. It seemed likely he would be released by the Premier League club he had signed for at 18; and, now that Luke needed him most, the agent (who had subsequently 'passed Luke on' to another member of his company's staff) ceased all contact. Luke tried on several occasions to contact him and his colleagues, but they became increasingly slow to respond. In short, Luke had been abandoned. All the enticing promises made in that initial meeting now appeared false.

Now, while Luke understandably felt wronged by his agent for not fulfilling his obligations, he could not justifiably blame him for the state of his career –

no matter how good an agent may appear or claim to be, he or she is only as good as the player they represent. If the player is not doing the business on the pitch then it is hard for the agent to deliver for him off it. But there is no excuse for an agent failing to return calls, or failing to do his very best for a player while he is under contract. Not only does an agent have a contractual obligation to fulfil his duties by working to the best of his ability for his players (as is covered in the next chapter), but – I believe – they also have a moral obligation too. This is someone's livelihood we are talking about, and it should never be taken lightly.

Nowadays, some agencies use ex-players as a means to recruit young stars. It could be argued that somebody who has played the game at a high level may relate better to the player's emotional and physical needs than someone who hasn't. This may be true; but I would strongly recommend that you be careful not to be influenced by an ex-pro's 'star quality'. I wouldn't necessarily buy a car because Lewis Hamilton is telling me I have to have it!

Adam Osper of London & Capital, a leading independent wealth management firm offering financial advice to many of the leading professional footballers in the UK, counsels as follows:

"Work with professional companies who are open, honest and transparent with you, whether this be your agent, lawyer, accountant or investment manager.

If anyone comes to you with something that sounds too good to be true... it probably is!"

Complete transparency

The current regulations around the payment of agents, by both clubs and players, are far more stringent than in days of old. There is a great deal more paperwork in place than when I began working in the business in 1998. In many ways this is a good thing: back then, it was widely believed that some agents were 'double charging' players for their services. While their Representation Agreements clearly stated that these agents would only charge a player for securing a deal when the club were not prepared to meet the agent's fees, some agents did not honour this clause – instead, they would hide the fact that the club had paid them once, and would then go to the player and ask for their fee from them, too. The agent would work on the assumption that the player would not bother to communicate with the club regarding agent's fees, and would just pay the full amount requested upon receipt of the agent's invoice.

And we wonder why us agents get bad press!!

Some agents even tried charging their player a percentage of his bonuses – which, as mentioned in the next chapter, contravenes FA legislation under Clause 7 of the player/agent Representation Agreement. Another 'convenient' way for an agent to siphon money from a player during a contract negotiation was by claiming that the club had only paid half of the stated 5% commission to the agent, and that this needed to be topped up by the player.

These days there is far greater transparency. The relevant paperwork must be signed by both the player and the agent, confirming whether the agent's services have been used, whether this was on behalf of the club or the player, and how much is to be paid to the agent. In other words, the player is clearly exposed to information on how much the agent is earning, so there can be no ambiguity. This paperwork is also submitted to the FA, and monies paid by clubs to agents have to pass through an FA Clearing House first. This level of organisation is, for the most part, cleaning out the agents who are less ethical when it comes to charging fees.

Communication is key

The world would be a boring place if everyone thought and acted in the same way, like robots. Every footballer is different when it comes to communication. Some like to have daily contact with their agent. Others are quite happy just to get on with it. This latter type of footballer will work hard in training, take care of his own finances and life off the pitch, and just call on the services of his agent when he needs assistance in securing a new deal.

As far as my business is concerned, I pride myself on offering a highly personalised, bespoke service to each and every one of my clients. I like to get to know them as people, and build a relationship that extends beyond the realms of just work. In this way, my clients get to know me personally, and vice versa, so we have more to talk about than just business. Hopefully, then, they feel comfortable chatting to me on whatever level they like. I have often received calls from clients early in the morning, on a weekend, or late in the evening because – for example – they are bored or frustrated, or because they wish to share some exciting news, like their partner having become pregnant. Those calls are always great to receive, because they show how much the player values their relationship with me, and that it extends further than just business.

At the same time, of course, it is important to respect peoples' boundaries, and appreciate the fact that some players are more private than others, and may not want that level of openness. I can work either way: the service I provide is tailor-made to suit the client, so that ultimately they know that, first and foremost, I have their best interests at heart.

This is where communication plays a vital role. The agent is there to help the player to achieve his goals. Unless those goals are communicated well, it is hard for the agent to deliver the correct advice. Likewise, this applies to the player's parents. From the outset of the relationship it is crucial for both parties to communicate well. For the parents, it's very important that you set out the parameters of what you expect from an agent, and ask as many questions as you can, until you feel certain that the agent is the right one for your son. Good communication leads to rapport and trust –both essential ingredients when selecting an agent to do the best for your boy.

Frank openness from the outset also allows you to predict more accurately whether an agent will stick to his commitments. I hear so many stories of agents promising the world, then delivering anything but. At the very least, an agent should make the calls they say they will; send information on time (contracts, insurance documents, financial information and so on); be in regular contact, both on the phone and in person; and provide constructive feedback.

On the matter of feedback, I know that some players only like to hear the good stuff, but my approach is different. I believe it is important to be completely honest with my players and their parents, and to make them realise from the outset that this is a very subjective business: not everyone will like or rate you highly, so you have to be open to criticism. Even negative feedback from a club can be useful if it helps to eliminate that club as a potential employer, or if it helps the player improve his game by taking criticism in a constructive manner. As the great American basketball player, Michael Jordan, once said:

"I've missed more than 9000 shots in my career. I've lost almost 300 games. 26 times, I've been trusted to take the game winning shot and missed. I've failed over and over and over again in my life. And that is why I succeed."

Take your time

There should be no unreasonable time constraints placed on you to choose the services of an agent. It is often best to 'shop around,' to get a feel for what's out there. What is key to remember is that an agent can only do so much for a player: injury aside, the destiny of a player lies at his own two feet. With that in mind, though, hopefully the agent you select will deliver what he promises, and be someone you and your son feel comfortable with, leading to a long and fruitful alliance.

Legally, an agent is only allowed to sign a player to a Representation Agreement when he is sixteen (and at that age this agreement must be signed by the player's guardian, too). Ross Wilson, at Watford, talked to me about the stage at which he feels that a player should have an agent:

"Personally, and as a club, I don't believe a player requires an agent until after he has signed his first professional contract at Watford. This is mainly because all scholarship contracts and first professional contracts at the club are the same for all of the boys.

However... this depends on the individual's situation and there are cases – such as when a player experiences an accelerated opportunity to develop through the first team, or if there may be other clubs looking to buy the player – [where] he may require the services and guidance of an agent."

Wilson's comments are supported by David Burke. Now Head of Football Operations at Brighton and Hove Albion FC, Burke has spent much of his career in youth football, at Fulham, Charlton and the ASPIRE School For Sporting Excellence in Qatar. In that time, he has worked with players such as Matthew Briggs (Fulham), Michael Turner (Sunderland), Mark Hudson (Cardiff City) and Darren Pratley (Swansea City). David believes that:

"There is no specific age that I would say a player requires the services of an agent, but rather [he needs one] when he is in demand, and [when] the parents are ignorant of the game. Ideally this would be on the player's second contract. Possibly if agents could not be paid until then, they would not target kids so young."

Any agent that pressurises you into signing a contract (be that a Representation Agreement or Playing Contract) is likely to be placing their own needs ahead of yours.

Dealing with agents at this stage, it is advisable to ask for recommendations and referrals from fellow players or their parents, and senior professionals. Look to players that you know and trust, and those who have achieved similar goals to your son's in their careers. The senior pros are likely to have a more informed opinion than your child's peer group, due to their greater experience and exposure to agents, and their connection to the football 'rumour-mill'.

Football agents work in a service-oriented industry, and much of our business is generated by word of mouth, goodwill and solid referrals. By the same token, it is widely known which agents have a poor reputation. Do your research and stay clear of them! Apart from the fact that you will probably be treated badly by these agents, some clubs will simply not deal with them, making their role totally redundant.

Be loyal

Competition is fierce within the agency world. You'll find that rival agents may try to lure your son away by claiming to be able to deliver a better service than his current agent. Many will belittle and criticise your existing agent in order to create a feeling of dissatisfaction. It is very easy for others to cast aspersions on your agent and make false claims, and there may be times when you find credibility in what is said to you. But if your son has signed a Representation Agreement with an agent, then honour it. Work together with that agent. Tell any other agents that approach you that you already have representation. It is actually a contravention of FA regulations for a licensed agent to:

"...induce a player or Club to breach his or its Representation Contract with another authorised agent or his or its Contract with another Club or player"
(Clause H.6.c of The FA Football agents Regulations)

The same regulations (which can be found on the FA website at http://www.thefa.com) also obligate the player to honour his Representation Agreement.

"A player must ensure that the exclusivity of any Representation Contract entered into with an Authorised agent is respected."
(Clause I.4 of The FA Football agents Regulations)

From my own point of view, alongside the contractual obligation, I also believe that, as an agent, I have a moral obligation to do what is right, fair and in the best interests of my client. In return, I expect a similar level of morality from that player.

We live in a society that hides all too often behind the saying, "it's nothing personal, it's just business"; but I'm a firm believer that who you are and the way that you conduct yourself shows up in every aspect of your life, be that with friends, family or business colleagues. Who you are in business is who you are in life. Don't hide behind excuses: just do what is right!

There is no price that can be attached to loyalty. And, sadly, there have been numerous cases of players who believed that 'the grass was greener', only later to find themselves in a worse position.

What if you choose badly and wish to get out of the agent representation agreement?

As discussed in Chapter One, selecting an agent can be a confusing process. In most cases you will be committed to a two-year contract, so it is natural to worry about the consequences of making the 'wrong' choice. It is important to note that the contract length is negotiable, so if you don't feel comfortable with this period of time, say so, and ask for it to be reduced.

You may well find that, after several months, the relationship just isn't working out. Perhaps the promises made in that initial meeting just haven't been honoured. If this is the case, you may request to be released from the Representation Agreement. However, unless the agent has committed a 'material breach of contract' (and there is normally a clause within the agreement that allows for the agent to rectify any breach he may have committed, provided it is done within a specified timeframe), it is extremely difficult, if not impossible, to cancel the agreement if the agent does not consent to do so. This is why I recommend that you research and deliberate thoroughly before making a commitment. Once you have made your decision, have the Representation Agreement checked over by a solicitor before you sign it.

I am not trying to instil fear and doubt here – rather, I'm just trying to highlight the importance of a little caution. Signing for an agent should leave you feeling happy and safe in the knowledge that you are going to be totally taken care of.

So: what if you do make that mistake, and sign with someone who you come to believe is not fulfilling their obligations?

Well, you can try coming to a resolution with the agent in an attempt to part company amicably. In my opinion, it is always best to be direct with your son's agent before looking elsewhere. If you have an issue, flag it early on in the relationship, before it becomes a big deal – at least give the agent an opportunity to set things right. Often, the agent may be unaware that you have a problem with them, so if you want it dealt with, tell them about it!

After all - if they don't know, they won't fix it.

If, however, the same problems keep rearing their head, there is help out there. You can always contact the PFA (the Players' Football Association, discussed further in Chapter 2), the union for professional footballers. The PFA offers free advice and deals with a number of issues, including supporting and defending players in times of dispute with their clubs. Bear in mind, though, that Representation Agreements are watertight, so beyond offering you advice, there is little the PFA or anyone else can do in terms of terminating a contract.

Still: there's no need to fret. Remember that you're only tied into the contract for a short period of time (two years maximum). So if you do have a bad time with an agent, just put this down to experience. Learn from your mistakes, so that you can make sure the potential pitfalls don't happen again with your next representative. Please don't allow one poor experience to cloud your general opinion of agents. There is such a thing as a 'good agent'.

In fact, there are plenty of us!

SUMMARY

£	Don't rush into signing with an agent. Meet a few and get to know them first
£	Pick someone who you believe is honest and hardworking (ask senior professionals for referrals/opinions on those agents that interest you)
£	Don't be cajoled into signing for an agent because they might offer to buy your son boots, or claim to represent top players. Such things are irrelevant. Instead, focus on what the agent will do for your son's career
£	Keep an open dialogue with agents. Good communication, trust, honesty and respect are the basis of any solid, long-term relationship
£	Be loyal to your agent and honour the Representation Agreement.

CHAPTER 2
REPRESENTATION AGREEMENTS

> **❝** I want the focus to be on my clients and not on me. **❞**
> Drew Rosenhaus - leading agent of NFL players

How the agent gets paid

Within the terms of the contract, there will be a clause stating how much the player is due to pay the agent. In common practice the agent only receives payment from the player upon concluding a contract negotiation with his club, or when the player transfers elsewhere. This payment is in the form of a commission - a percentage of the guaranteed gross income of the player. Some of the more unscrupulous agents have, however, been known to include bonus payments made to players in the calculation of their commission, but this is totally in breach of regulation. Agents are only entitled to a percentage of 'guaranteed' income as their commission, such guaranteed income consisting of:
(i) Basic gross salary
(ii) Signing-on fees.

The player and the agent will agree upon the agent's percentage, and this will also be stated clearly in the contract. The industry norm is 5%, but some agents charge more, and some slightly less. There is of course the odd horror story – there was one well-known case within the industry where a foreign agent who was supposedly 'looking after' a player that he had brought to the UK was charging his client an outrageous 25% of his guaranteed income! This was tantamount to genuine exploitation.

Julian Rhodes of Bradford City told me of an incident that he'd experienced a few years ago, where an unscrupulous agent put his own wants ahead of the needs of his client:

"When we (Bradford) were in the Championship League, we were trying to sign a player. He was offered more money by another club, but his agent told us that if we paid the agent more money he'd get the player to sign for us for less. Not only is this despicable behaviour, but it goes back to my point about why the player should pay the agent directly – if he is contractually obliged to pay him a fixed percentage of his earnings, then it is in the best interest of the agent to maximise the player's deal."

While the public consensus seems to be that football agents charge whopping fees, it is clear from the figures (a standard fee of 5%) that this is not the case – especially when you take into consideration the additional support services that a good agent provides. In fact, 5% could be perceived as a moderate amount compared to the 10%-15% fees common in other entertainment industries.

How and when commissions are paid to the agent

The majority of agents have a standard clause in their representation agreements stating that they only charge players in the event of being unable to claim their fee directly from the club. In most instances, the agent will inform the player that his club will be covering the fee, therefore nullifying the player's need to pay the agent directly. This is something that Julian Rhodes doesn't agree with – and, many might argue, justifiably so. While this setup sounds fantastic (a great service from a connected person who can get your son where he dreams of playing, and all for free!) the reality is slightly different.

When a player signs a Representation Agreement with an agent that is correctly submitted to the FA within the required five-day window (from the date on which the player signs to the date that the contract is received by the FA), copies are then stamped and returned to the agent and the player, subject to the agreement being approved by the FA. The agent is required to send three copies of the signed agreement to the English FA. The agent now officially represents the player, and this scenario is not without financial consequences. For example: in the event of a player signing for a new club that pays the agent's fee, this signing is officially documented and submitted to the FA. Even though the agent is being paid by the club, not directly by the player, his payment will be listed as a 'benefit in kind' on the player's P11D form. This means that the player will incur a tax charge on the agent's fees. At the time of writing, this tax charge is

40% of whatever the agent receives from the club. While this is arguably more cost effective than having to pay the agent the full 5% fee directly, many agents fail to mention this cost at all to prospective clients, either before the player signs with the agent or when the player signs for the new club. This means the player receives a larger than anticipated tax bill, months or even years later, and is left feeling cheated when they should have been made aware from the start.

During the process of drawing up the Representation Agreement, the player and agent settle on and document how the commission to the agent should be paid. There is either the option of a lump sum payment at the start of the employment contract or, more commonly, the agent is paid in equal instalments that are usually spread over the duration of the playing contract. This option can either be arranged through the club, so that the agent's fees are taken directly from the player's salary, or set up without any direct involvement of the club.

In all instances, relevant paperwork should be signed when the player signs his contract with the club, and disclosed at this point to the FA.

Unscrupulous agents

While the majority of agents are law-abiding, there are the odd few who will do whatever it takes to seduce players into signing with them. There have been cases where agents have enticed a player by offering him or his family monetary incentives, cars – even houses! This is illegal (as outlined in rule H14 of the FA Football Agents Regulations). Besides, if this situation occurs for you, you need to ask yourself a simple question: "does an agent that offers bribes have your best interests at heart?"

Then, when you have done that, ask this question too: "is it possible that this agent might conduct themselves in a similarly unethical manner in the future, putting my son at legal or financial risk?"

Who can act as an agent?

It is a fact not widely known that it is not only licensed agents who can act on a football player's behalf: in actuality, a player can also appoint a lawyer, or even a close relation, as an alternative.

As previously mentioned, an agent must be licensed – that is to say, the agent must be cleared by the Football Association. The FA will only approve an agent upon completion of a CRB (Criminal Records Bureau) check, and subject to the agent passing the agent's examination and providing proof of having taken the required level of liability insurance cover. Any agent who has done all this and who is properly licensed should have an official FA Agent's Number, so remember to ask for this as evidence that they are indeed 'kosher'. Note that the Agent's Number is usually the first letter of their surname followed by three numbers.

A lawyer does not need to take the agent's examination, but is required to register with the FA if he or she wishes to represent players. Needless to say, if you are interested in signing with a lawyer, it is therefore wise to check that the lawyer is registered with the FA.

Finally, a close relation must be a parent, guardian or sibling of the player if they are to act as a representative. The role of a close relation as an agent is limited to acting for the player or players to whom they are related, and they are prohibited from receiving any form of direct or indirect payment from the player or his club.

A close relation must submit an RCR (Registered Close Relation) Declaration Form (otherwise known as an AG6 Form with the FA) within five days of signing, in order to represent a player. This form is a very straightforward document. For access to this document, go to the FA website: www.thefa.com.

There have been a few examples of close relations acting on behalf of players, some good and some bad. The most famous is probably the case of the disruptive and unsettling influence of Nicolas Anelka's brothers. In the summer of 1999, when Anelka had only been at Arsenal for one and a half seasons, his brothers – also his representatives – were allegedly touting him all over Europe. The likes of Marseille, Real Madrid, Juventus and Lazio were all linked with the prodigiously talented star. By the end of that summer, he had moved to Real Madrid for £23.5 million.

While these events might not seem strange initially, a further look at Anelka's career suggests otherwise: the player has on average stayed no longer than two seasons at any one club for which he has signed (the exception being Chelsea). This is despite playing for nine different clubs in a 15-year professional career to date, and having signed a seven-year contract with Real Madrid in 1999. Anelka currently ranks third in world football's list of players who have accrued the greatest overall amount of transfer fees throughout their careers. Only Fernando Torres and Robbie Keane have transferred for more.

While nobody can claim that Anelka has not had an incredibly successful career in respect of earnings and trophies[1], there will always be the argument

---

[1] His career has included victories in Euro Championships at both Under-18 and full international level, the Confederations Cup, the English Premier League and FA Cup, the Turkish League Championship and the Champions League, as well as a PFA Young Player of the Year award

that his brothers influenced him to move for his and their own financial gain, rather than for the good of his playing career.

In my time, I have seen many parents who have tried to avoid using an agent by representing their son themselves. Sadly, in most instances this has led to tension between the player and their parent, and has often resulted in the player signing a less lucrative deal than that which an agent could have negotiated. It is not a slur on the parent, who clearly has their child's best interests at heart, to say that problems inevitably arise when a parent is unfamiliar with the rules and regulations, and with what should or should not be in a player's contract. A good, experienced agent, on the other hand, will deal with such things as a matter of routine. Think about it this way: if you needed your house rewired, would you forego professional help and tackle the job yourself? I'm guessing that, unless you're a particularly confident DIY'er, the answer is no! You would surely be far better off – both in terms of peace of mind and of preserving your health – if you paid a skilled electrician to do that job for you.

Despite this, though, there is nothing to say that once an agent is appointed, a parent can't still be involved in the negotiation process. In my own representative work, I think it is very important indeed to collaborate with the player and his guardian, especially before speaking to a club on their behalf. Every step of the way, the player and his support network should be kept fully informed of all events during negotiations, and invited to contribute.

The PFA

The PFA (Professional Footballers Association) is one of the oldest trade unions in the world. Formed in 1907, it serves to protect the rights and status of all professional players, through the use of collective bargaining agreements. Collective bargaining is a process of negotiations between employers and a group of employees aimed at reaching agreements that regulate working conditions. In such bargaining processes, the employees' interests are commonly presented by representatives of a trade union to which those employees belong. The collective agreements reached by these negotiations usually set out wage scales, working hours, training approaches, health and safety regulations, overtime, grievance mechanisms and rights to participate in workplace or company affairs.

The PFA plays a very important role in the protection of players' rights. I have often called upon the services of Simon Barker or Richard Jobson – an extremely affable pair – at the PFA, and they have always been excellent at helping resolve issues that my players experience with their clubs.

While the PFA also provides a service for negotiating players' contracts, they seem nowadays to play an ever-diminishing role in contract negotiations, because the status quo among players is to use an agent for this. This trend may be due to the popular perception of the PFA as an organisation set on achieving harmony within the industry. This means that they are perceived as less likely than an agent to push a club for a more lucrative deal for a player (after all, the agent is incentivised by the fact that he will earn more from a deal that is better for the player). I am not sure that this belief is correct, though: I am a huge fan of the PFA, and don't necessarily agree with some of the claims that have been levied against it as regards its involvement in player representation.

What a player/agent Representation Agreement looks like

A standard Football Association (FA) player/agent Representation Agreement contains 31 clauses (a copy of the standard contract can be seen at the back of the book in the Appendix section) or downloaded from the FA website, at www.thefa.com. Some clauses are obligatory, and others can be added to suit.

Some agents will add clauses without your knowledge, so do make sure – as you should with any contract – that you read through it very carefully. If there is anything that you don't understand, bring this up with the agent.

I strongly recommend in all cases that you always take independent legal advice before signing a contract. Along these lines, FA-approved contracts must now have a page (Appendix 1) in addition to the 31 clauses, to be signed by the player and/or his guardian if the player is a minor, confirming that they have had the opportunity to take legal advice prior to signing.

So, let's take a look at the contract in its entirety, and explain what it all means in simple terms. The standard FA Representation Agreement between an agent and a player can be found at the back of the book, in the Appendix section.

Clause 1. Appointment

Within this clause, the player and his guardian need to confirm whether their relationship with the agent will be 'exclusive' or 'non-exclusive'. Quite simply, this means that they either hand over full control of their Playing

Contract negotiations to the agent, or they do not. In the latter case, they are then able to appoint additional agents. I know of very few agents who will work on a non-exclusive basis, because this kind of arrangement will give them less control.

Clause 2. Term

Within this section, the duration of the Representation Agreement should be clearly stated. The maximum length permitted is two years. The Agreement can be renewed at any time during the two-year period, but cannot be extended for longer than two years from the date of signature. However, please note that the contract term can be anything up to two years that is agreed between the agent and the player – so don't be fooled into thinking you must sign for the full two years.

Clauses 3-6. Nature of the Relationship

Clause 3 is an extension of Clause 1, and only applies if both parties have agreed that the Representation Agreement is 'exclusive'. It states that the player will only use the services of the Authorised Agent during the period of the Agreement.

Likewise, Clause 5 is an extension of Clause 1 and only applies if both parties have agreed that the Representation Agreement is 'non-exclusive'. It states that the player is not restricted to using only the services of the Authorised Agent.

Clause 6 states that, regardless of whether a player is working with an agent on an exclusive or non-exclusive basis, he maintains the right to represent himself during negotiations instead of his agent. However, it is worth noting that most agents will insert a clause that, if this happens, the agent is still entitled to his commission as set out in Clause 7 (Remuneration); and if this is the case, why not use the skills of the professional, if you have to pay regardless? Makes sense, doesn't it?!

Clause 7. Remuneration

This clause sets out when the player will pay the agent, and how much he will have to pay. If the representative of the player is a solicitor, then he or she may charge an hourly rate. Most authorised agents charge a percentage fee for their services.

Percentages in the business vary, but it has become common practice to charge between 5 and 10% of the player's guaranteed basic wage. I have known of agents that have suggested they are entitled to a percentage of their player's bonuses (appearance money, promotion bonuses, etc.), but this is illegal (as confirmed under Clause G.8. of the FA Football Agents Regulations). So if an agent tries this, they are breaking the rules and ripping you off!

Clauses 8 & 9

Clauses 8 & 9 are optional.

Clause 8 states that the agent's commission must be requested from the player in writing, and an invoice provided.

Clause 9 says that the agent is responsible for all expenses incurred as a result of fulfilling his duties, and that these costs may only be passed onto the player if stated in the Representation Agreement. Note that it is not common practice for an agent to demand expenses incurred as it is widely recognised that the majority of work undertaken by the agent is speculative.

Clause 10. Obligations (on the part of the agent)

Clause 10 lays out the requirement of the agent to act in the best interest of the player at all times. It details such commitments as:

- The agent will not enter into negotiations with any other third party (be it another agent or club, the player's existing club, or a commercial enterprise) without the consent of the player.
- The agent will honour the rules and regulations of the FA, hold a valid license, and refrain from making illegal payments to a club to facilitate a deal.

Clause 11. Obligations (on the part of the player)

Clause 11 lays out the requirement of the player to honour the terms of the Representation Agreement and comply with the rules and regulations of the FA:
- The player is not permitted to have a pre-existing agreement with any other agent.

- If the agent is signed on an exclusive basis, the player will inform the agent of any approach by another agent or club
- If the player decides to use the services of another agent or represent himself, he must inform the agent of this in writing within five days.

Clause 12. Player consent

This clause simply confirms that the player has authorised the agent to act on his behalf.

Clauses 13-16. Termination

Clause 13 enables the player to leave the agent immediately should the agent have his license removed by the FA or FIFA.

Clause 14 allows for either the agent or the player to terminate the Agreement in each of the following three scenarios:
1. Either party commits a 'material breach' that can't be remedied
2. Either party commits a breach which isn't remedied within 30 days of receiving a written request to terminate the contract
3. Either party is declared bankrupt.

Clause 15 explains that any monies owed to the agent by the player need not be paid in the event of the Agreement being terminated due to a contravention of either Clauses 13 or 14.

To illustrate the effect of these clauses: In July 2010, a fictional player called Simon Allen moves on a free transfer from Stockdale County to Melchester United. Simon's agent concludes a deal where Simon receives £100,000 per annum in guaranteed income for four years and, in accordance with their Representation Agreement, the agent charges Simon 5% of his guaranteed income – a total of £20,000. Simon and the agent agree that such fees are to be paid in equal instalments on January 1st of each of the next four years – i.e. £5,000 per year. Simon pays the agent £5,000 in January 2011. In February 2011, however, the agent is found to have committed an offence that leads to his license being revoked by the FA. Simon then exercises Clause 13 of the Representation Agreement and immediately severs all ties with the agent. He is no longer required to pay the £5,000 per annum for the remaining three years of his contract.

Clause 16 gives the player three options in the event of the agent leaving

the organisation for which he may work at the time of signing the agreement. In this instance, the player can choose from the following options:
(i) To continue to work with the agent under the same Representation Agreement, but within the confines of the restrictive covenants placed upon the agent by his current employer
(ii) Sever all ties with the agent and sign with another agent from the same company
(iii) Terminate the contract and sign a Representation Agreement with another agent (this may be an agent that works independently or one that works for another sports management company).

The player must confirm his choice within 28 days of receiving notice from the agent of their change in circumstances.

Clauses 17 & 18. Notices (to terminate the Agreement)

Clauses 17 and 18 define the protocols regarding how notice to terminate the Agreement may be given by either party.

They state that this is relevant to players who are represented by an agent who works for a Sports Management company.

Clause 19. Severability

Clause 19 states that in the event of a clause in the Representation Agreement being illegal, it must be removed. However, this does not have any bearing on the validity of the rest of the Agreement, nor does it confer a right to termination.

Clause 20. Confidentiality

Clause 20 implies that both the player and the agent are bound to confidentiality with regards to the contents of the Representation Agreement and any other information in respect of contract negotiations and discussions with clubs.

Clauses 21 - 23. Entire agreement

These clauses set out to clarify that any discussions prior to signing the Representation Agreement are superseded by the agreement itself. This includes any fraudulent claims made by either party prior to signing. Furthermore, these clauses state that the Representation Agreement is complete and cannot be amended unless both parties agree to amendments in writing.

Clause 24. Relationship between the parties

This clause gives the player peace of mind, by dictating that the agent is prohibited from signing contracts on behalf of the player.

Clauses 25 & 26. Survival of rights, duties and obligations

These clauses state that, in the event of the Representation Agreement being terminated (whether through breach of contract or natural expiry), each party is still liable for claims against them by the other.

Clause 27. Non-assignment

This clause prohibits the agent from deferring his responsibilities as outlined in the Representation Agreement onto any other party without prior consent from the player. Furthermore, it states that the agent will not devolve any responsibility onto an unlicensed agent.

Clause 28. Third party rights

Clause 28 confirms that, under the Contracts Act 1999, any person not signed to the Representation Agreement has no right to enforce any of its terms.

Clause 29. Supplemental agreements

Clause 29 states that any other agreements in place between the player and agent must conform with the Agents' Regulations as set out by the FA, and must be submitted to the FA together with the Representation Agreement for registration. This also applies to 'commercial contracts' (as explained later in this chapter).

Clause 30. Disputes

Clause 30 informs both parties of the procedures for raising disputes that arise as a result of a breach of the Representation Agreement. Initially, a letter highlighting the issue and requesting resolution must be sent to the FA. If required, the FA will then refer the case to FIFA (the world governing body for football). In most cases, however, the FA will deal with the matter themselves.

If the problem between the player and the agent lies outside the realms of the Representation Agreement, then the matter will be referred to Arbitration, under Rule K of the Rules of the Football Association.

Clause 31. Governing law and jurisdiction

Finally, Clause 31 explains that the Representation Contract is governed and interpreted in accordance with the laws of England and Wales.

Key terms summary, Signatures and Appendix 1 – Independent legal advice confirmation

The key terms should be summarised at the start of the Representation Agreement. This summary consists of the names of the player and the agent/close relation/lawyer; a description of the services that the agent/close relation/lawyer commits to delivering; whether or not the agent/close relation/lawyer has been appointed by the player on an exclusive or non-exclusive basis; how long the contract will last; how fees are to be paid; and when fees are to be paid.

On the second-to-last page there is the provision for all to sign. A player under the age of 18 must have a guardian sign the contract on his behalf.

The final page (entitled Appendix 1) also requires signature from the player and guardian (if the player is under the age of 18), confirming that the opportunity to take legal advice on the Representation Agreement has been considered.

Once again, I cannot urge you strongly enough to have your Agreement checked over by a lawyer. At the time, it may seem like an unnecessary expense, but it is a small price to pay for long-term peace of mind that your son isn't being taken for a ride.

Commercial contracts

My stance on commercial contracts for fledgling professional footballers couldn't be more transparent: a commercial deal should be the furthest thing from your boy's mind as he tries to carve out a successful professional career.

Any commercial opportunities that come his way should be viewed as a 'bonus', but they should not be sought after. In my opinion, many opportunities for financial gain at such a young age should be deliberately avoided, in order to keep the player's feet firmly on the ground, and his focus purely on training and performing at his best in games. There will be plenty of time in the future for supplementary income from commercial ventures.

This notwithstanding, it is still wise to educate yourself, so as to be prepared in case your agent does approach you with a commercial opportunity.

Most agents will not only have a Representation Agreement with a player, but a Commercial Agreement too. It is common practice for an agent to charge around 20% for any commercial opportunities that they create for a player – a substantial cut, but arguably a justified one, as the player would not, in most cases, have secured the deal without the agent's help.

Sometimes an agent may be able to source commercial opportunities for players through advertising and promotion of sportswear. Nowadays, however, very few sportswear companies will pay a retainer for having a player on their books, and especially not a young one. The industry has seen quite substantial cut-backs, so unless you are a top-level professional like Stephen Gerrard or Wayne Rooney, it is unlikely that you will receive payment for wearing merchandise and apparel. What normally happens is that the likes of Nike, Puma, Adidas, Reebok, Umbro, etc. may provide young players that interest them with boots, goalkeeper gloves and other accessories, or maybe with a budget to spend in their stores each year.

SUMMARY

- £ Make sure that the agent is licensed or a qualified solicitor
- £ The contract must contain all obligatory clauses as per the Standard Football Association (FA) Representation Contract.
- £ Contracts must be lodged in triplicate to the English FA within 5 days of signature.
- £ A Representation Contract or Exempt Solicitors Terms of Representation is limited to a maximum period of 2 years
- £ The Player must be given reasonable opportunity to take independent legal advice and take advice from the PFA (Professional Footballers Association) prior to providing his written consent. Furthermore, the Player must provide written consent for the Authorised Agent to enter into a Representation Contract with the Club on the proposed terms and lodge the relevant player consent disclosure form with The Football Association.
- £ Standard practise in the industry is for an Agent to charge a Player between 5-10% of their guaranteed income upon concluding negotiations of a playing contract.
- £ Most agents procure their fees from the Club but the Player is liable for 40% tax on whatever sum the Agent receives.
- £ Agents normally charge the Player 20% of any commercial income generated.

CHAPTER 3
SCHOLARSHIPS

> **“** Somewhere along the line you've got to do your apprenticeship. **”**
> Alan Shearer - former Newcastle United and England striker

Some players are scouted at five or six years of age, and can be affiliated to a professional football club from as young as seven. If these players develop as expected, they may play for the club as a schoolboy and may ultimately be offered a scholarship, which is normally signed prior to the player turning 16, but which doesn't commence until the season that the player is 16 years of age.

A scholarship agreement is normally for two or three years, but it is possible for a player to sign a professional contract on his seventeenth birthday. The player can be offered the professional contract prior to turning seventeen, but it cannot be signed and activated until his seventeenth birthday. There are though, certain regulations governing when this can be done: the player must be offered a professional contract no sooner than 1st January in the year following the commencement of his Under-16 season.

For example: "Lee O'Donoghue" is a highly rated forward who plays for Chelsea. Lee was born on 22nd February 1997; therefore, he can only be offered the opportunity to agree, in principle, to sign a professional contract with the club on 1st January 2013. However, Lee must still wait until his seventeenth birthday (22nd February 2014) before he can actually sign the professional contract.

In special circumstances, a player may be offered a one-year scholarship agreement that automatically converts into a professional contract when that player turns seventeen. It is very likely that this was the case for such highly-rated players as Wayne Rooney and Jack Rodwell at Everton. A club will normally try to tie down a player considered a particularly 'valuable asset' as early as possible, in order to make the player feel wanted, and, more importantly, to fend off any interest in him from other clubs.

It is important to note also that contracts signed by players under the age of 18 cannot be for longer than three years.

Travelling time and distance becomes redundant

As you may be aware, your son must live within one hour's travelling time of his Academy or School of Excellence from the under-9 through to the under-12 age groups. Between the under-14 and under-16 age groups, this is extended to one and a half hours' travelling time.

Despite this, there are opportunities for players between the under-14 and under-16 groups to sign for clubs that do not meet this criterion, as long as the clubs fulfil their obligations under FA rules to provide the correct levels of coaching, education and welfare. For this reason, for example, in 2010 Raheem Sterling was permitted to transfer from Queens Park Rangers to Liverpool, despite only being 15 years of age. For those of you unfamiliar with UK geography, Liverpool's Academy training facilities are over 200 miles from those of QPR – an estimated journey time by car of at least three hours.

Please note that these travelling time regulations are the ruling at the time of writing, but from next season (the 2012-2013 season), new regulations will be in place that negate the travel time and distance ruling for all ages. For more info on this, see the section on the Elite player Performance Plan (EPPP) discussed later in this chapter.

The scholarship process

So, your boy's 15 years old and it's 'that time.' Will he be offered a scholarship, or won't he?

I don't envy players or parents who are waiting to hear the 'big decision'. This can be a really stressful time for a young man – not only does he have to work hard in training and perform in games, but he has to deal with the added pressure of revising for GCSE exams and completing course work. It is critical that a player doesn't neglect his education: there are no guarantees whatsoever that he will make it as a professional footballer.

Some clubs are very good when it comes to informing players about whether they will be offered a scholarship. They keep the parents and the players fully informed during the decision-making process. Others aren't so forthcoming with information, and leave both the player and his parents wondering what the future holds. Many families will be reluctant to request a quick answer, for fear of this having a negative impact on the club's decision.

Ross Wilson has dealt with releasing players at Falkirk and Watford. He joined Watford in the summer of 2011 in part because he was attracted by the new club's ethos of nurturing and developing young players through their Academy system and into the First Team. Since 1998, Watford has been incredibly successful with this business model: since that date, at time of writing, over 50 home-grown players have made their debuts for the first team. Such players include Adrian Mariappa, Lloyd Doyley, Scott Loach, Ashley Young and Marvin Sordell (with Young and Sordell currently playing in the Premier League, at Manchester United and Bolton Wanderers respectively). Wilson believes that Watford are very transparent in their dealings with players and their families when it comes to the 'crunch time' of discovering whether a scholarship contract will be offered.

"If a player isn't getting a scholarship then they generally know pretty early on. We are very transparent in how we deal with young players. We are constantly reviewing their development, assessing their progress and advising them on which areas of their game they need to work on to get to their end goal – being awarded a scholarship contract at Watford. If they aren't developing as we hoped they would then a clear picture is mapped out. It shouldn't come as any big surprise if they are told that they will be released, as we are continuously reinforcing to them which areas of their game require improvement."

I would always encourage a player, and his parents, to engage in open and frank conversation with the decision-maker at their club, and to request transparency regarding the club's intentions. In this way, if a scholarship is not going to be offered, the player is given the earliest possible chance to make contact with other clubs that may offer a scholarship or trial opportunity. Most clubs are responsive to this open approach, and want to help their players to progress, even if it is not to be under their tuition. Steve Beaglehole, Development Coach at Leicester City FC and former Under-19 and Under-21 Northern Ireland National Team Coach, acknowledges the dilemma set up by unclear lines of communication between parents and Coaches/Academy Directors.

"I believe that feedback is so important, and that the parents should be encouraged to ask the coaches how their boy is doing, and why he might not be in the team. But this depends on what type of coach you are.

I like to think that I'm very approachable [as a coach]. I openly admit, as a parent of a young player that has failed, I failed him as a parent. I should have sourced [the problem] myself more at the time. I didn't question why he wasn't playing more, or developing technically."

In my own work, a problem I have encountered several times occurs when a club is not sure whether or not to offer a player a scholarship, and takes until the very last moment before making and revealing their decision. This is a problematic position, as it may leave a player who does not receive an offer without enough time at the end of the season to seek out alternative opportunities, and to attempt to secure the all-important scholarship somewhere else. Such players then find themselves in limbo, without a club, during the summer period.

I feel that it is only right and fair for a club to inform a player and his family at the earliest opportunity if the player is to be released, in order to give him enough time to find something elsewhere. Similarly, the same should apply if the jury is still out on offering a player a scholarship for the following season: ultimately, the welfare of the player should come first. Steve Beaglehole concurs:

"I think it should be a ruling that every kid should be told by the end of the year in which their scholarship/ professional contract is due to be offered, whether he's getting one or not. I can understand if a boy has been brought into the club at the age of 15 why they may need a bit more time to assess him, but for me, there is no excuse when dealing with a player that has been with the club since the age of 12 or even younger."

When representing a young player, it is my policy to contact the club in January of the year in which he is eligible for a scholarship, to gauge the club's view on how the player is progressing, and to try to assess his likelihood of being offered a scholarship contract.

While all clubs must in any event notify a player of their intentions in writing by 1st March in the player's under-16 year, by this stage many players will have already been informed that they will not be offered scholarships. These released players will therefore benefit from a head start on finding an alternative club, and this is why I think it is so crucial to discover the club's intentions at the earliest opportunity. If it's a "sorry, but no," then you can avoid the 'rat race' and the pressure that comes with trying to secure another club at short notice.

When is a scholarship contract offered to a player?

Although some clubs drag their feet, revealing their decision at the very last moment, in accordance with FA regulations a club can offer a scholarship to a player on or after 1st January in the year in which he turns fourteen. This is done by completing a Form 33, which is then submitted to the Football Association.

Once the form is completed, the player then has 28 days to consider the offer made to him, before responding in Form 34. If he fails to respond, then he is considered to have rejected the offer.

In the event of the player accepting the offer, the Scholarship Agreement G(4) Form is signed by the club and sent to the FA in order to register the player as a scholar. This form is submitted together with the player's birth certificate and Scholarship Agreement.

When a player can trial at another club

A player can go on trial at another club only when:
- Permission is given by the club at which he is registered
- His registered club informs him in writing that they will not be offering him a scholarship
- 1st March of the relevant year has passed and the club has not offered him a scholarship contract in writing.

For example: 'Jon Kent,' a 15 year old player due to turn 16 in March, has been offered a scholarship contract by his club, Leeds Dynamos, but would like the opportunity to look at other clubs; but Jon would need to get permission from Leeds Dynamos in order to go on trial.

In accordance with Rule N.62 of the Premier League Regulations, any player who has received notification from his club to either retain or terminate his registration on or before the third Saturday in April (in the year that his registration is due to expire) is able to seek a move to another club. This, however, is under the condition that their current club is notified by 30th April and subject to approval, in writing, from the Secretary of the club that the player is currently registered with. However, if in Jon's case he hadn't been offered a scholarship with Leeds Dynamos by 1st March of his Under-16 season then, in accordance with rule N.63 of the Premier League Regulations, he would be free to seek registration as a student at another club from that moment.

Beware of the vultures

A player is most at risk from circling vultures between the ages of 14 and 18. By 'vultures,' I mean those agents and scouts who hover around players and their families as if the player is a piece of meat to be preyed upon.

I don't see any problem with a player and his family getting to know and trust the advice of an agent over a period of time. However, as we have seen, a player cannot legally sign a Representation Agreement prior to turning sixteen, and it is also illegal for scouts of other clubs to approach a young player or his family without first receiving permission from the player's current club.

For this reason, many clubs have resorted to only allowing family members to view Under-16 games: a sad indictment of where our game has got to, especially for those diehard fans who want to see the next Joe Cole or Jack Wilshere coming through the ranks. Some youth match grounds nowadays resemble high security military bases. UFO conspiracy theorists would probably surmise that the examination of an alien aircraft was being carried out there, instead of an innocent football match!

I can understand the paranoia to a degree, especially when you look at some past examples of players who have been lured away from their clubs. Possibly the most high-profile example in recent years was that of Chelsea being accused by Ken Bates, Chairman of Leeds United, of 'tapping up' two up-and-coming young stars of Leeds Academy, Tom Taiwo and Michael Woods. Apart from Mr Bates's misgivings regarding Chelsea's behaviour, a deeper-lying concern should probably be whether the move to Chelsea was in fact the best thing for these two young players' development. With hindsight, it can absolutely be argued that it wasn't. Taiwo failed to break into the Chelsea first team (no great failure when international stars are ahead of you in the pecking order) and is now plying his trade at Carlisle United in League 1. Woods, who is still contracted to Chelsea, is unlikely to progress into the first team, and spent a relatively unsuccessful loan spell at Notts County. Leeds might argue that, had they remained, the pair would have progressed into their first team and established themselves as Championship League players; but there are no guarantees to that either.

There are so many factors that determine the career progression of a young player. Some players show great promise at a young age but fail to blossom as adults. Cruelly, some have their chance taken away by serious injury. For a fantastic example of what is achievable, you only have to look at Jonathan Howson at Norwich City. Jonathan earned his move to the Premier League side by emerging through the same youth system that found and began developing Taiwo and Woods at Leeds United; unlike them, Howson remained at Leeds, pushing through the ranks into the first team and playing 185 times prior to his transfer to Norwich in January 2012 for around £2 million.

Conversely, the case of Oliver Hotchkiss – an exciting and highly sought-after prospect at the age of 15 – is less positive. With the likes of Sunderland, Middlesbrough and Newcastle all chasing his signature on scholarship forms, he eventually opted to sign for Leeds, where he became an example of a player who failed to deliver on his early promise. Oliver is now playing at Garforth Town FC.

Inducements are illegal!

In accordance with Rule N.90 of the Premier League, no club is allowed to induce a player to sign with their Academy or Centre of Excellence by offering any financial incentives. This restriction applies to all English clubs (plus Cardiff and Swansea in Wales), including those outside of the Premier League.

It has been alleged, however, that players – in particular foreign schoolboys – have frequently been enticed by several top European clubs that offer benefits to the players and their family members.

Dealing with being released by a club

It can be heartbreaking for a young lad of 16, or even 18, to be told "sorry, we aren't going to be keeping you on or offering you a contract." They may have been at the club since the age of eight, and they might have many players, coaches and backroom staff as friends there. The rejection can have a devastating effect on a player – indeed, in some cases I have known of lads to give up playing altogether at this point. This is very sad – there is no way they would have lasted that long at a professional club if they didn't have talent, and to give up is tragic.

On the other hand, some players use this rejection as a driving force to prove the decision-makers wrong, and this is exactly the sort of attitude that must be displayed by a young player endeavouring to make it as a professional footballer, especially at the highest level. Your son will always encounter doubters and critics - football, after all, is a very subjective business.

I regularly remind my players that football is about proving people wrong. In this business players must constantly respond to their critics. Even the likes of Darren Bent have had to do this in their careers. Darren is someone who scored goals for fun at all levels while playing for Ipswich – first as a youngster, then as a reserve team player, and eventually as a first team regular in the Championship. A move to Charlton in the Premier League saw no let-up in his goals-to-game ratio, and he earned a big-money move to Tottenham Hotspur. Despite maintaining a one-in-two goal-to-game scoring ratio, he was somehow deemed not good enough by many Tottenham fans, and he struggled to force his way into the England set-up. Rather than let the experience quell his enthusiasm, however, he set about proving people wrong, at Sunderland and now at Aston Villa, where he maintains an excellent goalscoring record. There will always be doubters who believe Bent is not good enough to pull on an England shirt, or that he is unworthy of the large transfer fees that he has commanded – but he doesn't let this stop him from banging in the goals. Darren Bent is just one high-level example of a player with the mental toughness to keep proving people wrong.

A club's perspective on releasing players

The experience of telling players that they're surplus to requirements is not just traumatic for the players. It can also be heart-wrenching for those at the club who have to deliver the news to the boys – some of whom they have worked with for many years, growing very fond of them. It is an extremely sensitive issue for clubs to address.

When it comes to identifying and nurturing young prospects, Des Bulpin is one of the best coaches around. Des has overseen the development of over £90 million worth of talent, including Ledley King at Tottenham Hotspur, Dan Gosling at Plymouth, and Peter Crouch, Nigel Quashie and Kevin Gallen at QPR. Des has also been Assistant to Gerry Francis at Tottenham and QPR, Assistant to Ian Holloway at Plymouth and Leicester, National Team Manager in the Philippines, and National Under-21 Manager in India. Needless to say, he has a vast amount of experience of working with youth players. Des claims that:

> "Lots of clubs release players by letter, but this is wrong. It absolutely has to be done one-to-one, in person, and with the parent of the child present too, even if that player has only been at the club on trial. The lad should always be

told the truth – i.e. why he isn't being taken on, and what he lacks. He should also be directed into the path of another club – for example, a lower league or even non-league club. I would always give a boy the name of a club and the Manager there. I'd also provide him with that Manager's number, and say that [the Manager] could always speak to me about the lad. The reasons why I would do this are threefold:

1. Most importantly, it is the right and proper thing to do. The child deserves the truth.
2. He also deserves an opportunity somewhere else.
3. If I'm not sure whether he may or may not be good enough, I could always keep an eye on him and follow up on his progress.

I always tell the boys that I release that I could be wrong in my decision, and that they should go away and prove me wrong. The key to success is the hours spent practicing. Players are not born, they are made. It's about practice and good decision-making."

A key to releasing young players properly is the 'after sales service' that clubs provide in helping a player find alternative employment. Some clubs are great at actively sourcing opportunities elsewhere; but in my experience, many, if not the majority, are not so accommodating. Perhaps this is due to lack of time and resources, but unfortunately I also believe it is often the case that clubs don't wish to experience the embarrassment of having a released player making a success of himself at another club. Time and time again, I have witnessed clubs making decisions about whether or not to retain players so late in the season that there is little or no opportunity for the players to seek trials and secure a contract elsewhere for the following season. This leaves the player in limbo throughout the summer, and at a huge disadvantage relative to those whose clubs have been decent enough to release them early.

There are some clubs that are very helpful in assisting players to secure a new club; but in my experience, the majority are not. A rare positive example with one of my own clients is that of Dean Furman when at Chelsea. With the aid of Brendan Rodgers and Neil Bath (respectively the Chelsea Youth Team Manager and Academy Manager at that time), Dean was helped to remain in the professional game. He was informed in advance that he was unlikely to be awarded a professional contract at Chelsea, and both Brendan and Neil utilised their contacts in Scotland, working with me to help Dean secure trials at both Celtic and Rangers. Dean (see picture section) later went on to sign for Glasgow Rangers.

A situation like this, when the club is acting slowly to the player's potential detriment, is one in which an agent plays a pivotal role by applying a little pressure to the club to provide an early decision. In my experience, it is far harder for the player or his family to do this: they find themselves treading on eggshells, for fear of pushing too hard for an answer from the club.

While this is my observation, a general assessment of all the clubs in the country operating Academies or Centres of Excellence, there are of course many clubs that do right by the players. Watford is certainly one of those. At Watford, the system provides fair appraisals when releasing players, and provides them with help and the support they need to make progress in their lives, in whatever direction that may be. Ross Wilson of Watford explains:

"When it comes to releasing a schoolboy, the Academy Manager, Assistant Academy Manager and Coach are all there to inform the player and his parents of their decision and reasons why. The player should already be aware of the reasons due to the clear and transparent way in which we at Watford communicate regularly to the players what is required of them to improve their skills. We would always invite players back in to meet with the Welfare Officer, and chat about what they might want to do next in their lives, be that seeking a scholarship or pro contract elsewhere, going to university, or perhaps looking to attend College in the US. We provide a support process that helps the players put something in place beyond their time at Watford.

When an 18-year-old scholar or pro is being released, the First Team Manager, Academy Manager, Development Coach and I are all there to give the player the news. We always try to be fair and honest in our appraisal with that player, and not to give him false hope should we feel that he doesn't have a career in the game, or that he won't play at the level he believes he can. By the same token, we will also advise players who might not think that they have a future in the game [if] we do not believe this is the case, and encourage them to continue to pursue a career as a professional footballer."

The agent's role when a player is released by a club

Along with the contract negotiation process, the unfortunate situation of being released is one when an agent can have undeniable value to a player, stepping in to provide support that is especially important if the club falls short in this regard.

It is important to get this right. Although these teen years are a relatively brief part of a player's career, I cannot over-stress the importance of that extra year of development in the right environment and under the correct tuition. While in England we now see Under-16s and Under-18s football, Scotland has retained the Under-17s and Under-19s age groups that used to be the norm in England. While this might not at first seem significant, this apparently subtle difference has a detrimental effect on many players south of the border, while opening up opportunities in Scotland. This is because some players are later developers than others, both physically and mentally: 17- or 18-year-old players may be equipped to compete against other lads of their age, but when they are thrust into older men's football, many struggle with the physical aspect of the game. Along with the scrapping of reserve team football, this restructuring of the age groups in the English game has created a situation where boys of 18 are being forced into first-team football, with nowhere else to develop their skills.

The 'player development' problem caused in part by this shift in age groups has now been widely recognised, with the introduction by some clubs of an Under-21 development squad. The hope is that this innovation will enable some players to gain the extra year or two that they so desperately require in order to make the step up to the next level.

In the meantime, what does a released player do when he does not have the support of his previous club in finding somewhere else to continue his career progression? If he has chosen his agent wisely, he turns to his agent. This is a challenge that presents itself to a lot of players; and without the help of an agent to promote their skills to other clubs, it is extremely difficult for them to facilitate transfers or trial opportunities.

For this reason alone, it is vital to have an agent.

SUMMARY

- £ Scholarship contracts start in the season following a player turning 16 years of age.
- £ Scholarship contracts are generally for a period of 2-3 years.
- £ These can be offered at anytime on or after a player turns 14 years of age
- £ Try finding out as early as possible (ideally no later than January in the year in which a player turns 16) whether or not he is going to be offered a scholarship by his club.
- £ If a scholarship contract has not been offered by 1st March in a player's final year as a schoolboy then he is free to go on trial at another club.
- £ It is illegal for a club to offer financial incentives to a schoolboy or his family in order to entice him away from his current club while registered with them.
- £ Don't let being released by a club be the end of your football career. Remain positive and confident in your ability and seek an alternative club.
- £ An agent is normally the best way to help find a new club.

CHAPTER 4
MOVING CLUBS - TIME FOR A FRESH START

> **❝** Change brings opportunity. **❞**
> Nido Qubein

Taking one step back to take three steps forward

Many scenarios can present themselves to the young footballer seeking a career at the top level. Your son may be lucky enough to be at one of the top six Premier League clubs, and the thought of being a professional at Manchester United, Chelsea, Liverpool, Manchester City, Arsenal or Tottenham Hotspur may well be a dream come true to a young man.

It is advisable, though, to look at the bigger picture. Assess the medium- to long-term effects of signing for such a club.

I am not for a second implying that you steer clear of them, but consider this: if your son has set himself a goal to play first team football at the age of 18, he may well have to reassess where he signs – or adjust his goal to make it more realistic. This is, of course, unless your boy happens to be a talent of the stature of Wayne Rooney, Jack Rodwell, Andy Carroll or Jack Wilshere.

I am not suggesting that the likes of Gareth Bale and Theo Walcott wouldn't have broken into the first teams at Tottenham and Arsenal respectively had they come through their youth systems – but it is far more likely that they wouldn't have been regularly exposed to first team football as early in their careers if they had not been at a club further down the leagues like Southampton. It could be argued that Bale and Walcott are so good today precisely because they started their careers at a Championship League club with the ethos of developing 'home grown talent' into their first team.

In some instances, it may be advisable to adopt the approach of 'taking one step back in order to take three steps forward'. There have been many examples of players who've had to follow this route to the top, including Jimmy Bullard (released by West Ham), Jermaine Beckford (released by Chelsea), and David Platt (released by Manchester United). All of those players had to drop down several levels in order to play regular first team football.

In Jermaine Beckford's (see picture section) case, he did incredibly well to re-establish himself at Leeds United, having been away from the professional scene for three years, and having returned to it at the age of 22. Most players who reach the higher echelons of the game do so by finding a lower league professional team that provides them with early exposure to first team football; but in Jermaine's case, after being released from Chelsea at the age of nineteen, he went to a non-league, semi-pro side, Wealdstone. There he established himself as the most prolific goalscorer in the division, and soon scouts from all over the country were coming to watch him play. The great thing about Jermaine was his unwavering belief in his own ability. He always knew that he had the ability to compete with the best players in the country within his age group. With hard work, focus and incredible belief in his own talent, he has managed to prove his doubters at Chelsea wrong, and forge a very successful career for himself. I recall taking him up to Leeds on the day that he signed for the club, leaving his day job as a windscreen fitter for the RAC behind. That was a great day!

Biggest isn't always best!

So: while you may think that your son is best off at one of the biggest clubs in the country – Manchester United, Manchester City, Liverpool, Tottenham, Arsenal or Chelsea – the truth is that young players often have a greater chance of 'making it' at a smaller club where first team football is more attainable. After all, if you are performing well in the first team, at whatever level, you will soon be picked up by a larger club.

I think that it is a myth that the biggest clubs have all the best young players. It is certainly the case that the larger clubs have a greater number of scouts, and greater resources to help develop a player's career; but all too often at the top clubs there is a 'glass ceiling' between the youth and first teams. For a player in this situation, I would encourage signing for another club where he can see an unobstructed route into the first team – not least because of the additional barrier of big money foreign transfers standing in his way.

The likes of Manchester City and Chelsea routinely buy some of the best and most expensive players in the world – exciting for their fans, but no good for a young player aspiring to break through into the first team. In fact, the proof is in the pudding: how many players have forced their way through from the Youth Academy to the First Team at Manchester City or Chelsea in the last couple of seasons? The answer is two at Man City – Ben Mee and Dedryck Boyata – and three at Chelsea - Josh McEachran, Ryan Bertrand and Sam Hutchinson. This is in stark contrast to the likes of Watford (six by my counting) or Bradford City (seven).

As Peter Horne, Head of Youth Operations at Bradford, acknowledges,

"The big attraction for young kids here is that we have a proven track record of developing talent. Our record for turning youth players into established professional players is one of the best in the country... In the last three seasons we've had seven home grown players make their debuts."

While the figures listed above only account for the last two seasons at time of writing (the 2010-11 and 2011-12 seasons), and while a larger number of players have made first team debuts at the likes of Man City and Chelsea if you look at – say – the past four seasons, consider this: not since John Terry's debut in 1998 has another Chelsea player emerged through the ranks of the Youth Academy and maintained a regular place in the starting line-up, or even on the bench, for the first team. Similarly, at Man City, with the exception of Micah Richards (a client of ours), who made his debut in October 2005, no home-grown City player has managed to hold down a place in the first team.

In fact, of the team that won the FA Youth Cup for Man City in 2008, the likes of Keiran Trippier (Burnley), Ben Mee (Burnley), David Bell (Peterborough) and Daniel Sturridge (Chelsea) have all felt it necessary to leave the club in order to progress their careers by playing regular first team football elsewhere. Likewise, Dedryck Boyata (on loan at Bolton) and Vladimir Weiss (on loan at Espanyol), also key players in that successful team, have needed to seek moves that gave them an opportunity of first team football, because the chances of doing so at City were so limited.

Reserve team scrapped!

It used to be the norm for 17- or 18-year-old players to play reserve team football. The reserve team would be affiliated to a competitive Reserve

League that was split into two sections – the northern section and the southern section, or the eastern and western leagues – to save on travelling time and expenses to clubs. For example, during the 2009-2010 season there existed the Barclays Premier Reserve League South and North divisions. The Southern section would consist of the likes of West Ham, Arsenal, Chelsea, Portsmouth, Birmingham, Aston Villa, Wolves, Stoke (although I'm not quite sure how the last four, especially Stoke, managed to be classified as 'southern'), while the Northern Division comprised Hull, Manchester United, Manchester City, Blackburn, Burnley, Bolton, Everton, Liverpool, Wigan and Sunderland. This gave young players an opportunity to mix with senior pros, many of whom would have had first team experience. Equally, there were times when reserve matches were used as an opportunity for a First Team player to return from an injury lay-off and regain their match fitness (as Sol Campbell did at Arsenal when recovering from a calf injury in August 2005). Either way, younger players were given the opportunity to bridge the gap between Youth Team football and First Team football.

Unfortunately, the Reserve Premier League was effectively scrapped at the end of the 2009-10 season, and many lower divisions have followed suit. Many scouts argued that the reserve matches were a waste of time for them, as the senior professionals playing would simply "go through the motions", thereby making it difficult to refer or recommend players on the basis of reserve team performances. The general consensus among clubs was that the games were becoming a costly exercise that wasn't really beneficial, as many clubs pretty much played their under-18 team in the league, making some fixtures quite literally boys against men. Additionally, the obligation to fulfil Reserve Team fixtures as well as Youth Team and First Team matches meant that clubs often required larger squads. Eventually, most clubs played Youth Team players entirely, and so the Reserve Team game became merely another Youth Team fixture, which effectively led to the disbanding of the League.

What is more commonplace nowadays is the practice of clubs putting on 'friendly' matches, then inviting other managers and scouts to come and watch players they are interested in signing on a loan basis.

The problem with this scenario is the question of what happens to the players aged 17-18. While they get a great deal of experience playing competitive football within their own age group, when do they get the opportunity to impress the First Team Manager by playing with the senior professionals?

Going out on loan

It would seem that the directive imposed by the FA several years ago that reformed Under-17 and Under-19 youth football into Under-16 and Under-18 age groups has had pretty significant implications, compounded by the scrapping of regular reserve team fixtures as described. These changes have impacted the development of many players who now find it difficult to make the large leap from youth football into senior professional football, especially at the highest level. As a result, many of the more forward-thinking clubs have now begun implementing 'development squads' for players aged between 18 and 21, allowing these players to continue their career progression and mature at their own rate. Some players are later developers than others, and that extra year or so can prove vital to both their physical and their psychological growth.

At the time of writing, the problem associated with playing development squad games is that they are not part of a competitive league, and only involve players up to a certain age limit. It could be argued that this isn't a fair representation of the professional game, and therefore that it is not useful preparation for First Team football.

For this reason, I believe it is vitally important for a player to get out on loan at around the age of 18. Some players have done so prior to turning 18, and some have even been loaned before signing a professional contract (in this latter case, the process is classed as going on 'work experience' - as Steven Caulker did when loaned by Tottenham Hotspur to Yeovil in August 2009). Whether on loan or work experience, this coal-face exposure is invaluable. It gives the player an opportunity to play in front of a good-sized crowd, and to participate in games that have more at stake. There is no substitute for the pressure and excitement of a 'real match'. Going out on loan is often the making of a player. It can show the player's parent club that he has the ability to hold his own at that level, proving that he has matured as a player. For example, as Steve Beaglehole, Development Team Coach at Leicester City, told me:

> "Players need to be playing league football (or at least competitive football) when 18/19 years of age. Two of our boys have gone out on loan to Bristol Rovers this season, and it has brought them on leaps and bounds."

But going out on loan is not always easy. Managers are under extreme pressure to deliver results every week. Many would rather take a player with a proven track record in their club's division than give a chance to a younger, more inexperienced player.

I had this problem when I was looking after Adam Lallana (see picture section) at Southampton several years ago. At 18, I knew he was ready for a loan opportunity, and that he had all the ability needed to cope comfortably at League 1 level. I personally thought that he was ready for the First Team in the Championship, but clearly my opinion wasn't shared by his manager – it's a game of opinions! All Adam needed was the opportunity to prove that he was good enough. Regrettably for us – and, probably with hindsight, regrettably for the many managers to whom I spoke at the time – no-one would give Adam the platform on which to demonstrate his undoubted quality. As a result, he continued patiently to play reserve team football. Eventually, he got his opportunity with the First Team, grasped it with both hands, and hasn't looked back. I had no doubt then that he would star in the Premier League, and I remain completely faithful now that he will. It is just a shame that more people couldn't see that at the time when he most needed a break.

Compensation – a scary word!

At present, if a registered player at a club rejects a scholarship in order to move to another club, his original club is entitled to compensation for the training and development of the player. However, under the current system of compensation, many clubs feel short-changed. A good example of this was the movement of Jermaine Pennant from Notts County to Arsenal at 15 years of age. Despite Notts County receiving something in the region of £2million for him (a record fee for a trainee at the time), this was far less than the value that Notts County had placed on the player, leaving a bitter taste in the mouth for the club.

The amount of compensation offered in a case like this would normally be based on training and education costs, plus further payments upon the player making future first team and international appearances. An element of potential would also be taken into account when calculating the initial down payment. This type of cheap deal is potentially to the detriment of the original club, and is the reason why many clubs are so over-protective of their young stars, for fear of the bigger clubs coming in and poaching them.

While there doesn't appear to be any set compensation formula in place for these cases (as there is, for example, in the transfer of foreign players under UEFA guidelines), each case is looked at and judged on its own individual merits by the Professional Football Compensation Committee. The level of compensation awarded is often based on prior cases used as a precedent.

In many instances, however, the two clubs agree the level of compensation and structure of the deal. This is usually more heavily incentivised and rewarding for the club from which the player is moving, as they will receive further payments when the player fulfils his potential - i.e. if he reaches an agreed number of appearances for the new club's first team, plays for the national team, etc. The club of origin also usually stipulates receiving a percentage of any future transfer fee that the player commands.

Unless the player is an exceptional talent, I have found that many clubs are a bit wary of paying compensation fees, as the agreed figure is fixed and binding. Furthermore, the level at which compensation is set is unpredictable. As mentioned previously, each case is taken on its individual merits, and there is a lot of variation in compensation figures. Take, for example, the cases of Dan Harding, Daniel Sturridge and John Bostock.

Harding left Brighton and Hove Albion in 2005 to sign a three-year deal with Leeds United. At the time Harding, 21 years old, was out of contract with Brighton and rejected a new, improved offer from the club. This meant that Brighton was entitled to compensation for him. A fine prospect, Harding was on the cusp of a call-up to the England Under-21 squad on the back some strong performances for his club. He had been at Brighton from the age of 16, and the tribunal decided that the club were to be awarded £450,000 upon Harding signing for Leeds, plus a further £400,000 subject to first team appearances, international caps and promotion success, together with 20% of any transfer fee that Leeds received in the future should they decide to sell the player.

Sturridge was 20 years old when he transferred from Manchester City to Chelsea, having already established himself as an England U-21 international and having played 16 times for his club in the Premier League. The Professional Football Compensation Committee decided that the compensation package for him would be far greater than that awarded to Brighton for Dan Harding. Chelsea were ordered to pay an initial fee of £3.5 million with additional payments of £500,000 after his 10th, 20th, 30th and 40th appearances in the First Team, plus a 15% sell-on fee on his next transfer. Admittedly, Sturridge had been with City for a longer period of time than Harding had been with Albion, having signed for Man City when he was just 13 years old. He had also proven to be capable of playing in the Premier League at a tender age. Despite this, Harding had already played two full seasons in Brighton's first team, but commanded a compensation fee that was only one tenth of Sturridge's, despite being the same age.

There was much scrutiny over the decision to award Crystal Palace £700,000 in compensation when the highly rated 16-year-old Jonathan Bostock moved to Tottenham Hotspur in July 2008. At the time, Bostock was widely regarded as one of the best young talents in the country. Further add-ons to Palace amounted to £1.25 million dependent on appearances for Tottenham, and an additional £200,000 should the player receive a full England international cap. There was also a 15% sell-on clause in favour of Crystal Palace.

Bostock, of course, was younger than both Sturridge and Harding; but the differences in these examples still highlight the unpredictable nature of the compensation system, despite the official line of using previous cases as a precedent. This is why many clubs are scared to take cases to tribunal and why in most instances they try to settle the compensation package between themselves.

Precedents have been set by the compensation payments awarded when Tom Taiwo and Michael Woods moved to Chelsea from Leeds; when Louis Hutton and George Swann moved to Manchester City from Leeds; and when Luke Garbutt joined Everton from Leeds. The high levels of compensation awarded in those cases (especially those of the lads who went from Leeds to Chelsea) have led to a reluctance amongst many clubs to take the signing of a player to a Compensation Committee. The cases of Harding, Bostock and Sturridge go some way toward highlighting further why clubs are reluctant to go to tribunal. There is little guarantee that, under the current system, the selling club will receive the level of remuneration that they deem fair, but the buying clubs tend to be worried that they might end up paying 'over the odds'.

The new Elite Player Performance Plan is due to be launched at the start of the 2012-2013 season. One of its main purposes is to bring greater consistency to the compensation model – though this may not necessarily prove to be to the benefit of those lower league clubs, as explained later in this chapter.

When compensation is payable

Under current FIFA regulations, any club that has been involved with the training and development of a player from age 12-23 may lay claim to compensation:
(i) When the player signs his first professional contract
(ii) Each time he is transferred up to and until the end of the season during which he turns 23.

Elite Player Performance Plan (EPPP)

On Thursday 20th October 2011, the EPPP bill was passed by a majority vote among Football League clubs. The new system will see clubs' Academies and Centres of Excellence split into four categories, with the top Academies in the country holding the top 'Category 1' status. The key changes to the existing Academy system will be as follows:

- An increase in the amount of coaching time for players in Category 1 status Academies
- An increase in the annual payments to clubs for their youth development programmes
- The abolition of the transfer tribunal system, which will be replaced by a fixed level compensation system.

The EPPP is a dramatic reform that paves the way for clubs to match the model of training youngsters used with such sparkling success at Barcelona FC. Current rules limit coaching hours and travel distances for young players, but the EPPP aims to change all that.

Firstly, the EPPP is seeking to increase the current number of coaching hours per week for players aged 9-16 from five hours to between 15 and 20, putting English football on a par with other European countries in this regard. According to sport's journalist, Paul Fletcher, under the current academy system, by the time players reach the age of 21 they have usually received around 3,760 hours of professional coaching (BBC website on 15th February 2011); the EPPP would increase that to around 10,000, which will have an exponentially positive effect on the development of young players in England. In fact, this figure neatly mirrors Malcolm Gladwell's '10,000 hour rule' as described in his book Outliers, published in 2008 – a theory that one of the keys to success in any field is to practise a specific task for 10,000 hours.

Secondly, the EPPP aims to scrap the travel rule that currently only permits clubs to sign young players living within 90 minutes travelling distance from their training facilities. It is expected that this will lead to the bigger clubs recruiting young players from further afield, moving them into residential complexes near to their training facilities. This will allow the most promising players to train alongside each other – it seems logical that this can only be a positive move for those elite players.

Premier League clubs have been licking their lips in anticipation of the new EPPP regulations. The EPPP will lead to a simplified and standardized compensation system, making the prospect of signing a talented youngster from a lower league club that much easier and more predictable.

The virtues of this new system for the game overall are, however, debatable. I would argue that, in the long-term, lower league clubs that heavily rely on the development of young players (both to strengthen their first team and to create profit through selling them on to the bigger clubs) will suffer greatly. Crewe Alexandra, Swindon Town, Stockport County and Luton Town are just a few examples of clubs that have ensured their survival in recent years by developing home-grown players and selling them onto Premier and Championship League clubs.

Another problem for smaller clubs under the EPPP will be the difficulty in achieving Category 1 Academy status, due to the cost of the criteria that must be met in order to achieve it. These criteria include increases in the number of full-time Academy staff, and higher-quality for training facilities and equipment.

The new system will signal an end to the current trend of Premier League clubs paying large fees for the best young talent in the Football League: it will see the introduction of fixed tariffs. These will be calculated in accordance with how long a player has been at the selling club. Clubs will be paid £3,000 per year for every year of a player's development between the ages of nine and 11. The fee per year for players aged 12 to 16 will depend on the selling club's academy status within the four-tier system, and will range between £12,500 and £40,000.

This new system will therefore see an end to deals like the initial £600,000 fee that took 16-year-old Luke Garbutt from Leeds to Everton in 2009, or the move of 14-year-old MK Dons starlet Seyi Ojo to Liverpool, from which MK Dons are thought to have received around £2million . Under the new system, Ojo's transfer to Liverpool would have cost the Premier League club under £150,000 – a saving of £1.75 million!

How will the new system affect young players?

As with most regulation reforms, there are pros and cons to the new system. My own opinion is that, in the long-term, this new system will cost English football dearly. While I accept that the current compensation system is unpredictable and can be a deterrent to bigger clubs, it is nonetheless important that smaller clubs be fairly remunerated for the time, effort and costs involved in running a productive youth system. Indeed, without the correct levels of funding, I foresee many lower league clubs having to stop running a youth system entirely, particularly once the initial four-year additional funding (a condition of the new

EPPP system) from Premier League clubs to lower league clubs expires. In an interview on the BBC Sport website on 20th October 2011, Barry Fry, Director of Football at Peterborough United FC, concurred:

> "What frightens me is that a lot of clubs will pull out of having a youth system altogether. Lower league clubs will look at how much it costs to run their academy or school of excellence and think that, if the Premier League can nick their best players for a low price, what is the point of investing in it?"

Fry should know what he's talking about: he was responsible for structuring the deals that saw home-grown Peterborough talents Matthew Etherington and Simon Davies sold to Tottenham Hotspur in 2000, and Luke Steele to Manchester United in 2002, all of which are estimated to have generated Peterborough somewhere in the region of £6 million. This figure hugely exceeds what Peterborough could expect to have been paid under the newly structured compensation system.

It seems logical that a wave of clubs closing down their youth academies will hit British football hard. So what will the consequences be?

Obviously, there will be extremely limited spaces at the clubs that still operate youth academies. Perhaps even more detrimental, though, will be the increased likelihood of top-flight clubs splashing out, buying many young players for under £100,000 on the basis that they can afford for several to fall by the wayside, just as long as some succeed. In simple terms, young players will become more like pieces of meat that can be discarded with little consequence.

There will probably be a plethora of 18-21 year old players at Premier League clubs who will be unable to break into their first teams. As an additional twist, Premier League clubs almost always send such players out on loan to lower league clubs – a perverse quirk of fate that will further thwart the development of home-grown talent from the lower leagues.

On the other hand, Leicester City's Steve Beaglehole sees the positive aspects of the new system:

> "I think that EPPP is a positive move. It is now documented that 18-21 [year olds] have got to have 12 hours per week training which must be logged, monitored and audited, and this doesn't include game time. At the moment players are doing far less than that. I see this as being a major plus, and contributing to the 10,000 hour rule. I also think that bringing down the ratio of players to coaches means you'll see more quality training, as it will be far more personalised."

Steve Quashie, Head of Education & Welfare at Queens Park Rangers, agrees with Beaglehole. He thinks the EPPP will have a positive effect as far as the West London club is concerned.

"The EPPP will enable the club to attract better players, as in the short term we will become a Category 2 Academy. This will result in the club playing in a better games programme. Our long term plan is to become a Category 1 Academy – however this will only be possible when the club moves into a new training ground."

It might seem as though the so-called 'big clubs' would look favourably on the new EPPP system because of the perception that it will allow them to get players from lower league clubs more cheaply than under the current tribunal system; but this line of thinking (as adopted by Barry Fry) is not shared by the likes of Bradford City. Bradford have, in recent years, been prolific in developing and selling young players to help finance the club. As Chairman Julian Rhodes acknowledges,

"The Football League identified us as a club who would be against the new regulations, but we're not unhappy with the new EPPP system. We've all settled on extra money, which can only be beneficial for us. With solidarity payments coming in each year, money is being filtered down and at least it is guaranteed. Besides, I'm confident enough in the way we are doing things that we won't lose out. The only unfair element to this new system, I feel, is clubs who haven't historically produced players like we have still get as much as us."

Champions of the new system may argue that once it is in place, more players will have access to some of the best coaching in the country at the bigger clubs and, therefore, more players will have a better chance of reaching the very top of the game. However, others might suggest that this won't change anything – just look at the players who've been coached at top-flight clubs since the ages of eight or nine who have subsequently been released at 17 or 18. Sadly, many of these have been unable to secure a scholarship or professional contract at any Football League club.

I currently represent a young player who has been at excellent Academies, in Watford and Swansea, for nine years, since he was nine. Now, at the age of 18, he is battling to secure a contract at a non-league club. This is no reflection on his talent, but merely a reflection of the fact that there are so many players out there in a similar position. There is quite simply, more supply (players) than there is demand (spaces at clubs). I don't see how this will change under the new rules.

In fact, I'd argue that there may be greater long-term opportunities under the new system for most young players if they remain at lower league clubs. Here, they will be better placed to push their way into their first teams, and use that as a stepping-stone to the next level up, the 'big time'. This is in contrast to players who will see the bright lights of a big club at a tender age, move, and then find that their long-term development is stunted by being so far from the first team.

SUMMARY

- £ Don't be afraid, or too proud, to drop down to a lower level in order to play games. Use these games as a platform from which to progress to playing at a higher level
- £ Being signed to a smaller club gives you the opportunity to get valuable first team football at an early stage of your career
- £ If you're signed to a big club at 18 or 19, it may be wise to seek a loan opportunity, so as to get some first team experience – especially if your club doesn't operate a development squad
- £ Compensation is payable for the training and development of players between the ages of 12 and 23
- £ Many clubs are put off from paying compensation for a player. This is for fear of having to pay more at a tribunal than the figure they at which they value the player
- £ The new Elite Player Performance Plan (EPPP) comes into effect at the start of next season (2012-13). There is a mixture of support and opposition for the new system.

SHOW ME THE MON€Y!

PICTURE SECTION

South Africa and Leeds legend, Lucas Radebe, with adoring kids from the SOS Childrens Villages charity after playing in an Invitational International XI v Bafana Bafana All Stars match in 2005.

SHOW ME THE MONEY!

Jermaine Beckford winning the Mitre Goal of the Year Award at the 2008 Football League Awards for his goal v Rotherham on 17th February 2007, while on loan at Scunthorpe.

Dean Furman winning the Mitre Goal of the Year Award at the 2011 Football League Awards for his goal at Oldham v Notts County on 14th August 2010.

SHOW ME THE MONEY!

Craig Davies celebrating his second goal v Doncaster on 19th November 2011.

Adam Lallana after winning the Johnstones Paint Trophy Final with Southampton at Wembley Stadium on 28th March 2010.

CHAPTER 5
GOAL SETTING

> By recording your dreams and goals on paper, you set in motion the process of becoming the person you most want to be. Put your future in good hands — your own.
>
> Mark Victor Hansen

Setting clearly defined goals

"People with goals succeed because they know where they're going."
Earl Nightingale

The quote above expresses very simply why it is so important for your son to set goals in all areas of his life – and not just career and financial goals, but personal ones too. Clearly-defined goals will give him clarity and focus: he will know what he's aiming for, and when he does, he can then set objectives (stepping stones and minor goals) that lead to the ultimate goals. Some of these objectives may seem small. Make it into the starting line up for Saturday's game, for example, or get picked for an FA Youth Cup match in 3 weeks' time. Others will be bigger: play for the national team in the World Cup Finals. Whatever his goals may be, he is far more likely to achieve them if he writes them down and refers to them regularly.

Goals are well-defined statements of what we WILL do, not what we MIGHT do. Studies have shown that only 3% of us actually set goals. And how about this for a statistic: According to Gino Blefari, in Thoughts on

Leadership: Impact and goals on the road to success (January 6th 2011), on average, people who have written down their goals end up achieving 89 per cent of them, and earn on average ten times as much as the 97 per cent of people who do not write down goals.

Goals are the roadmap to success

Setting goals gives your son both long term vision and short term motivation. The very act of setting a goal is an incredibly positive process. Consigning it to writing makes it even stronger, by both reinforcing it and aiding the next process – taking action. There is no point in setting goals if all your son is going to do is admire the fact that he has set them. We've all heard the saying "actions speak louder than words", and it's true. The next stage is to make them happen.

On first meeting a prospective client, I always try to find out what their goals are. What are their ambitions? Where do they see themselves in 2 years, 5 years, 10 years and even 20 years time? I appreciate that many young men won't have given thought to their long-term goals, let alone set stepping-stone minor goals in order to fulfil those larger hopes and dreams. But 'hope' can be galvanised if we have a clear vision that is supported with a plan. Yes, your boy will need a little bit of luck along the way – but luck just stands for Labour Under Controlled Knowledge – work undertaken from what you already know. In other words, you literally make your own luck! This is why, with intelligent application, your boy may just find that his 'luck' improves out of sight.

David Burke stresses to me the importance of goal setting and using role models to achieve the results you desire:

> "I believe it is crucial that players have a role model to look up to and learn from, and that they also set themselves step-by-step goals to achieve whatever they want in their careers and lives."

So you want to be a player then, do you?

The next sections of this book are directed at your son. I would strongly urge him to read this book in its entirety, to familiarise himself with the 'football business,' but he should pay particular attention to the remainder of this chapter, and Chapters 6 and 7. They are especially for him!

What do you want to achieve in your playing career?

How can I possibly hope to get an A grade in a subject at school unless I work to achieve it? How can I achieve it without listening to what the teacher is saying, studying hard and completing my homework?

It's simple. I can't!

Football is no different. Unless you set out to become the best that you can be, then back that up with hard work, you will always fall short.

The best way to start the process of getting where you want to be as a player is to set clearly defined short-, medium- and long-term career goals. No matter how odd this may feel at first, I guarantee that you will achieve far greater success during your life if you complete this task. And I don't mean just writing them down to leave them somewhere to gather dust, never to be seen again: you must check on your goals regularly, especially the short term ones, and tick them off when you've accomplished them. I'm sure you'll agree that there's something deeply rewarding in being able to tick off a task or goal that you've achieved. You get a massive sense of pride by accomplishing it, and it gives you the self-belief that you can go on to achieve even greater things.

Your goals may change over time, and there's nothing wrong with that – so long as you don't sell yourself short.

There's a handy way of setting out your goals, too. Your goals should always be SMART – that is to say, Specific, Measurable, Achievable, Realistic and Time-framed.

A good example of the power of goal-setting is that of a player I represent, Craig Davies (see picture section). At the end of the 2009-10 season, Craig was released by Brighton and Hove Albion FC, who were in League 1 at the time. Having signed for League 2 side Chesterfield in the summer of 2010, Craig looked me in the eye and told me that his aim was to score between 15 and 20 goals that season. What happened next was a case of a man proving his doubters wrong in the most emphatic fashion. Craig didn't just achieve his personal goal-target, he surpassed it. He scored 25 times that season, helping Chesterfield gain promotion as Champions of League 2, was voted into the PFA 'League 2 Team of the Year,' and earned himself a transfer to Barnsley, in the Championship.

Don't just work hard, work harder than others

After you have set your SMART goals you need to map out clearly how you intend to achieve them. For example, you may aim to work an extra hour on the training field or in the gym every day, to improve your technique, strengthen the weaker areas of your game, or build up your physique to make you stronger and harder to push off the ball.

You may wish to consider this: on the basis that professional footballers train on average for around 2 hours per day (unless they do a double session), by training for one extra hour per day, you effectively accumulate two-and-a-half days worth of extra training for every five days that you train with the team. In essence, you are doing 50% more than other players. Do you not suppose that this will help you to markedly improve your game over a short period of time, giving you an advantage over those who train less?

I am not suggesting that this happens every week, week in week out, as rest is a vitally important part of training too. You must, of course, give your body sufficient time to recover from tough sessions and games, in order to recharge itself and be able to perform at peak levels. But it is not by chance that some of the best players in the world are also some of the hardest working!

I remember an occasion when I took a young player to Manchester United for a trial, in January 2008. We were given a tour of the training ground by a senior member of staff, who made it a point to impress upon my young client the importance of hard work. He asked if we could guess who were the three players from that squad that came in the earliest and stayed on the training ground the longest. His answer was Wayne Rooney, Paul Scholes and Cristiano Ronaldo – arguably the three most naturally gifted players at the club. His point couldn't have been clearer: the more you give, the greater you become. Success isn't just derived from pure talent. It has to be combined with hard work and the right attitude.

Steve Beaglehole at Leicester City told me this:

"More and more, we are looking at the character of players. Give me two players, one with exceptional talent but a poor attitude, and another with far less ability but a great attitude, and I'd be taking the latter all day long. One of the common denominators of players who make it in the professional game is a spot-on attitude."

Indeed, when I asked Ross Wilson, Peter Horne and David Burke what characteristics they look for in a player prior to signing him, the phrase that kept coming up was "having the right attitude".

There's a famous quote by Gary Player – the great South African golfer who won nine major championships and is widely regarded as one of the finest golfers of all time – which he borrowed from the American film producer, Samuel Goldwyn. Player said of his success, "the harder I practice, the luckier I get."

Reputation is key

During my 14 years in the game, I have known many talented players who have sadly not fulfilled their potential. For me, one of life's greatest tragedies is an individual who wastes their gifts. If you have the talent, you must use it, not just take it for granted. Please don't become one of those people who turns around in years to come and laments, "I was some player back then, if only I'd..." This phrase normally ends with - "...listened to the people who were trying to help me and had my best interests at heart", or "...worked harder" or "...not hung around with those friends I had at the time who were a bad influence on me," or maybe even "...not had such a stinking attitude."

I'm sure that you don't want to ever look back on your career with any regrets. Thankfully, avoiding this is simple. If you listen to your coaches, work hard, support your team-mates and play with a smile on your face, you will be regarded as the very model of what a young footballer should be. Trust me when I say that a good reputation is worth its weight in gold.

Unlike a good one, which must be forged over a long period of time, a bad reputation takes a second to get and a lifetime to get rid of. The business magnate Warren Buffet, one of the richest men in the world, agrees with this:

> "It takes 20 years to build a reputation and five minutes to ruin it. If you think about that, you'll do things differently."

In the case of Barnsley forward Craig Davies, this saying was something that well and truly came home to roost. Craig would be the first to hold his hands up and say that he didn't have the best attitude when he was a young player. Back then he frequently found himself in all kinds of minor trouble. Thankfully, though, he learnt the errors of his ways, and went on to mature into a dedicated professional; but convincing the people that matter (i.e. other managers) that he has changed is something that hasn't been easy. In these situations, a stigma becomes attached. Managers will routinely be advised to not touch the likes of Craig, the suggestion being that he's a "bad lad".

At 26, Craig is now a very different person to the young lad who used to get into trouble – mature, focused and determined to prove what he and I both know he is capable of – and thanks to the likes of John Sheridan at Chesterfield and Keith Hill at Barnsley, he has been given the chance to prove himself again. But for every Craig Davies there are probably five players with a poor reputation in the game who aren't fortunate enough to be given more chances to make it. Don't let that be you.

What do you want to achieve in your personal life?

It's important to remember why you are doing all of this.

When I say "all of this" I'm referring to entering into the football business. The 'funny old game' can be a rollercoaster ride of emotions, full of trials and tribulations, massive highs and lows. Some may find that daunting, while others may become energised and view it as an incredibly exciting challenge. Either way, I hope you're doing it for the right reasons.

Those reasons are personal to you. They may be as simple as a love of football and a dream to play for the club that you've supported all your life. It may be that you see football as a vehicle to earn some great money doing something you enjoy and are passionate about. On a psychological level, I would suggest it is important to get to the root of your 'why' – your main motivation for becoming a professional footballer. This will become the driving force that powers you towards achieving your goals.

I would encourage you to set goals for all that you aim to achieve in your personal life, not just your footballing career. Break these down into 'material' goals (cars, houses, clothes), lifestyle choices, and family ambitions (perhaps to get married and have kids, or to be able to support your parents and siblings). Perhaps even more rewarding is setting 'spiritual and emotional' goals – for example, donating regularly to charity, or attaching your name to an organisation that you are fond of, like Lucas Radebe (see picture section) does for FIFA as an Ambassador of SOS Children's Villages. Or maybe you'd like to give something back to the community, by operating soccer schools for kids from disadvantaged backgrounds. Perhaps you'd like to be a mentor to talented children who may have lost their way a little. Whatever your choice, it is good to have goals that stretch you beyond yourself. Staying connected to the 'real world' makes you that much more grateful for what you have, and gives you a sense of fulfilment from helping others who haven't had your opportunities.

And of course, don't forget to set simple financial goals. As with all of your

SMART goals, these must be realistic and achievable, and you should seek advice from specialists who can help you to invest (not just spend!) your money wisely.

A great example of good financial decision-making is Robbie Fowler. He earned some fantastic money in his career playing for the likes of Liverpool, Leeds, Manchester City and Blackburn in the Premier League; however, rather than waste it all on expensive cars, clothes and gambling, he invested it in property and other business ventures, and now has a reported wealth of around £28 million (Wikipedia). Rio Ferdinand is another example: he too has invested in a range of business interests outside of football, to supplement his income and ensure that he has a financial legacy when he retires from the game. In June 2011 he was listed by Companies House as having Directorship status in ten different companies ranging from charities to music and film production companies . These included Rio Ferdinand Live The Dream Trading Ltd; RGF Enterprises; White Chalk — Youths In The Basement Ltd; Rio Films LLP; Scion Films Sale and Leaseback Sixth LLP; Rio Ferdinand Live The Dream Foundation; White Chalk Publishing; White Chalk Records; Next Generation TV & Film Ltd; and Broomfield Business Ltd.

A friend in need is a friend indeed - committing to achieving your goals

As with training and playing, nobody can achieve your goals for you. You have to do this yourself.

Make no mistake, the only way that you'll reach your targets is if you fully commit to doing whatever is necessary in order to make them happen. It is widely accepted that those people who not only write down their goals, but also share them, are those who stand a far greater chance of achieving them. There are two simple reasons why this is the case.

The first is that a person who understands the importance of your goal will hold you accountable. Have you ever told someone that you were going to do something, and then not done it? Do you think that person had more or less respect for you after you failed to deliver on your word? Aren't they less likely to believe you the next time you say you'll do something? If you fail, you will start to lose credibility in their eyes, and embarrass yourself in the process. So once you have told them, it is quite likely you will do everything possible to avoid failing.

Secondly, that person is there to support you. If they suspect that you are slacking, they will be able to give you the proverbial kick up the backside or arm round the shoulder, or whatever may be needed to keep you on track.

We are the products of our thoughts

Without getting too deep into the subject and risking the accusation of being labelled a 'hippy', I believe in the Law of Attraction.

In essence, the Law of Attraction suggests that we can attract anything into our lives that we wish for, so long as we have unwavering belief and a clear vision. Furthermore, we must not only believe that we can achieve that thing but that we will achieve it; and we should live as though we already have it in our lives. For a more sophisticated explanation, I would strongly recommend watching the movie 'The Secret,' produced by Rhonda Byrne.

An example of this would be a footballer who has set a SMART goal of playing for the first team of his club, so he regularly visualises making his debut for the first team. Not only must he vividly picture it in his mind, but he must also make the experience as intense as possible: in his mind, he can feel the sensation of the crowd cheering as he is warming up on the touchline, focused on his job, while his manager gives him the instructions he needs before running onto the pitch. The more intense you make the experience in your mind, and the more regularly you practise it, the more likely it is to happen – especially when you compound the effect by setting your goal in writing, too. Psychologists believe that visualization establishes neural pathways in the brain that then act as a blueprint to be followed in the actual performance.

A perfect example of this effect is the case of British Athlete David Hemery. Before Hemery won the 400 metres hurdles Olympic gold medal at the 1968 Mexico Olympics, he visualized himself running the final in as many different circumstances as possible. In every instance he pictured himself winning the race. In his mind, he ran that race in every lane against every possible opponent, in every different type of weather condition, and several times in each case. By the time of the Olympic final, he had already won that race so many times in his head, his confidence was such that he felt all he needed to do was turn up and win it for real.

Vision boards

An extension of this visualisation concept is the use of vision boards. A vision board is simply a board or wall upon which you place a collage of images of things that you wish for in your life - this may range from your perfect car, to a home, or even a girl! The theory behind this is that by seeing the images on the board regularly enough, they become rooted in your subconscious mind, and eventually become a reality if you maintain the clear focus and vision required to attain them. In your case, for example, you might use a picture of a player in the shirt of the club you want to play for in the future.

SUMMARY

- £ Set clearly defined goals that are SMART
- £ Don't just list your career goals, but also your personal, spiritual and financial ones
- £ Write your goals down and read them regularly
- £ Put in the extra training time. There's no substitute for hard work
- £ A good reputation is essential
- £ Find someone close to you to confide in, someone who will hold you accountable to achieving your goals, and who will support you during tough times
- £ Practise using visualisation to help you achieve your goals.

SHOW ME THE MONEY!

CHAPTER 6
ACHIEVING GOALS THROUGH SELECTING GOOD MENTORS

> A mentor is someone whose hindsight can become your foresight.

Anonymous

Copy someone who's achieved what you want to achieve in the football world

Having a mentor or role model with experience in the game is an invaluable asset that enables you to learn from both the good and bad choices that they made during their career. If you mould your behaviour on theirs, and on the advice they give you, you are far more likely to have a successful career. This approach is also a way of fast tracking yourself to getting where you want to go. For this reason, you must pick your mentor wisely.

In the modern game, the likes of Frank Lampard and Paul Scholes are viewed as excellent role models. The way they live their lives both on and off the pitch is highly praised. They are both family men who work extra hard in training. This is why they have reached the top level of the game and maintained that level for so many years. You rarely, if ever, hear of them being disciplined by their club for bringing either the game or the name of the club into disrepute. They also don't get caught drinking and partying to excess when they should be concentrating on games, unlike some other so-called 'professionals'. Don't get me wrong, nobody is perfect – both have had their moments in the past – but these have been isolated incidents and not regular occurrences.

I once heard a story about Lampard from a player who was at Chelsea as a young lad. He had just finished his training session for the day when he noticed that the first team had also completed their day's work on the training field. All the players went inside for a shower and lunch but there on the main training pitch was the lonely figure of one player with a set of cones doing 'doggies'. It was Frank Lampard. This was a man who was, at that time, a Premier League and Football League Cup winner with Chelsea, the Barclays League Player of the Season, a runner-up as FIFA World Player of the Year, the Football Writers' Player of the Year, twice PFA fans' Player of the Year, and with 38 England caps to his name. Yet, despite all of this success, he still had the hunger to carry on putting in hard graft when everyone else had packed up for the day. Lampard hadn't forgotten what had made him great – hard work and extra training to ensure that he was the very best that he could be.

I would strongly recommend selecting a good mentor who you can mimic in order to achieve the goals you set for yourself. Ross Wilson strongly supports my claim that role models play a massive part in achieving success in whatever you do:

"It doesn't matter who you are in life, I believe that you should always follow excellent role models. If you follow the right role models then money will follow you, rather than you following the money."

Find someone at your club from whom to seek inspiration

Regardless of whether the first team place you are striving for is at Manchester United or Macclesfield Town, I would urge you to seek a mentor who is close to home, and ideally at your current club. This is because it will be easier to mirror this person on a daily basis, adopting the positive traits they possess and, in turn, mirroring their excellent results. As a bonus, this person will have specific knowledge of the club's culture, and will be able to point you in the right direction for success. For example, when they were both at Leeds United, there is no doubt that Jonathan Woodgate benefited hugely from playing alongside, and training daily with, a consummate professional and international defender like Lucas Radebe.

There are many fantastic characters in football who are willing to help young players by imparting their wisdom. I know it may sound old-fashioned, boring and just like the sort of thing you probably hear from your teachers and parents, but it is so true that the advice of those older than you should be respected. These guys have learned as much from their mistakes as from the right choices they have made in the game. There is no substitute for life experience and, more often than not, advice is given by people who want to help you because they care. My advice is to listen carefully and take on board what is being said. Don't decide to dismiss it. After all, they've already experienced what you're going through.

Read!!!

I have to admit to not being too keen on reading when I was at school. This was mainly because I associated reading with studying for academic subjects that didn't really interest me at the time. I found it a rather ironic choice of words whenever I was asked to "anal-yse" a piece of work.

Things change when you find a subject or person that you are interested in and can relate to, though. Reading becomes a completely different and enjoyable experience, and one that helps with your personal development.

For this reason, I'd encourage reading biographies and autobiographies of people that you respect and admire – ideally people who attained greatness in their particular field, so you can gain insight into how they have achieved their successes. The likes of Alan Shearer, Wayne Rooney or Roy Keane would be good examples. I would also encourage you to study successful people outside of football, such as Richard Branson, Robert Kiyosaki, Lance Armstrong, Sir Steve Redgrave and Tiger Woods.

It can also be equally valuable to read about somebody who has gone from the top of their field to an all-time low and endured pain and suffering in their lives, such as Paul Gascoigne, George Best or Stan Collymore. The lessons to be learned here are equally important: they will help you avoid falling into the same traps.

Mentors outside of football

There are no rules against having more than one mentor, or choosing ones that come from outside the world of football. A good mentor is somebody who inspires you, and whom you greatly respect because of what they have achieved in their lives and the way in which they conduct themselves. For example, you may be inspired by the heart, determination and perseverance of Lance Armstrong or Sir Steven Redgrave. Maybe the actors Will Smith or

SHOW ME THE MONEY!

Tom Hanks are role models to you, or possibly Bill Gates or Richard Branson, or Martin Luther King. It is great to have interests outside of football too – explore them, and explore the possibility of finding a mentor within these fields. Hopefully you will highlight some aspirations that you have not only in football, but in other businesses and in your personal life. Your mentors should be your inspiration and should provide benchmarks for achieving your targets. Copy their traits and habits and, sure enough, you will soon find that you'll be a step closer to fulfilling your own hopes and dreams.

Try not to burn your bridges

As you progress through the ranks of youth football, you'll soon begin to experience some of the politics involved in the game. In truth, this is really no different from any other workplace. Although they may deny it, coaches and managers will usually have their 'favourite' players. In some cases, these players may not have as much ability as you, but they'll still start in the team ahead of you. This is difficult to comprehend at a young age; but welcome to the world of 'business'.

There may be good reasons for this, even if you find it hard to agree with them: it may simply be that the player selected ahead of you has been training better, is better suited to the manager's playing system, has a stronger work ethic, or is more of a team player. Whatever the case, it is a game of opinions, and ultimately the only opinion that matters is that of your manager. He's the one that picks the team.

Additionally, have you ever noticed that when managers move clubs, they often sign players that they have worked with before? Success in any business is built on good relationships, and clearly in these cases the relationship between coach and player has been successful in the past to the extent that the manager feels he must have the player in his squad again.

Should an 'old favourite' be placed ahead of you in the pecking order, it is crucial that you deal with it as professionally as possible. Accept the disappointment of not being selected with dignity. If you genuinely feel that your situation is unjustified, perhaps approach the manager politely and ask for the reasoning behind his decision, and inquire about what you need to improve on to increase your chances of selection. Please though – whatever you do – don't go throwing your toys out of the pram. If you start shouting and screaming or go into a big sulk and adopt an 'I don't care' attitude, this will be picked up on very quickly. You will demonstrate an inability to take constructive criticism and improve your game. Not a good look.

It is critical that you don't make enemies of coaches and managers because, quite simply, you never know where they might end up, or when you might need them to put a good word in for you. Football is a global business, but a village industry. Trust me when I say that everyone knows everyone in football. You may have heard of the 'six degrees of separation' – the idea that everyone is approximately six steps or fewer away from any other person on Earth? Well, in the football business, this can be adjusted to the 'three degrees of separation' theory!

It never ceases to amaze me how many times young players have become the subject of interest at a club that has an old coach of theirs in their staff. Now, if the old coach thought that the player had a poor attitude when he was younger, he might warn the current Manager off signing the player, and if the feedback is poor then the Manager is likely to be put off (as mentioned, this was historically a problem for Craig Davies, and for many others like him). But if the feedback is good, then the opposite is true.

This is why I strongly urge you always to be polite, courteous and hard-working, wherever you are. You may work with coaches that you don't like, but that doesn't mean you have to express your dislike or – even worse – make it public knowledge. Keep the channels of communication open, respect the fact that these coaches are just doing their job, and get on with doing yours. If the feedback on you is, "he wasn't a moment's trouble, he's a great trainer and nice lad, I just didn't think he was good enough," then the opportunities to prove that you are good enough will present themselves easily. But if your reference reads "don't touch him, he's a bad lad and a destructive influence," then you'll be cursing yourself for scoring an own-goal. You never know when you might need somebody's help in the future.

SUMMARY

- £ Select mentors that you can copy to achieve your goals. This is the best way to fast track your success
- £ Look for successful role models in professional football, and also people outside of the football world who have traits that you wish to adopt
- £ As well as studying those who've enjoyed great success, read and learn about those who have struggled, so as to avoid making their mistakes (Paul Gascoigne or Mike Tyson, for example)
- £ Always be polite and respectful to your coaches and fellow players, so that future feedback is always positive.

CHAPTER 7
WORK HARD ON YOURSELF

> **❝** Don't wish it were easier, wish you were better. **❞**
>
> Jim Rohn

Personal development

I am a great believer in the power of personal development and a mentally positive attitude in all aspects of life. In the highly competitive world of football, where players may be best of friends off the pitch, yet vying for the same position on it, you need to have confidence in your own ability. After a poor performance in a game or a lacklustre training session, this can be hard to maintain. Even more testing can be a prolonged recovery from serious injury, or the experience of taking a barrage of abuse from fans – or possibly even from your manager! During these challenging times, it is essential that you remain positive about yourself and your ability. There are many things that you can do to help with this, but listening to motivational CDs and watching inspiring movies or Youtube clips is a great place to start.

At the time of writing, Linford Christie is the only British man to have won gold medals in all four of the major competitions open to British athletes: The Olympic Games (1992), The World Championships (1993), The European Championships (1986, 1990 & 1994) and The Commonwealth Games (1990 & 1994). Christie was an advocate of something called PMA: Positive Mental Attitude.

Cynics may say that this 'PMA' was just a catchy slogan contrived by an advertising company to help sell a famous cereal brand; but it held true to Linford's approach towards running, and it brought him great success. He was always very positive about himself and never shy to reinforce the notion publicly that he was the best. He used to say that before each race he would enter a state of "tunnel vision" – his entire focus would be on his lane, blocking out everything else around him (competitors, fans, conditions, etc.) in the lead up to and during each of his races. The essence of Linford's technique was this: concentrate on yourself, and don't worry about what others are doing. Linford's lesson is a valuable one to anybody in competitive sport.

Your focus should be purely on being the best footballer that you can possibly be.

Mental/psychological development

As we know, it is important to keep yourself as positive as possible – but don't be under any illusions. At times it will be tough. There may be moments when you question whether all the hard work and frustration is worth it. Let me assure you, though: the rewards can be great – and not just in a financial sense.

How does this sound to you: being stuck behind a desk for eight hours a day, doing the same mundane tasks, day in, day out, week after week, year after year, living for your weekends and the 20 days of holiday that your company gives you each year?

Sound good?

I didn't think so!

Okay then, what about this: spending 2-3 hours per day doing something that you're passionate about and love doing, would normally do with your friends in your free time, and actually get paid (sometimes very handsomely) for it?

It's a no-brainer, right?

And – by the way – I've not even begun to depict an image of what a really bad job can be, I was just talking about a standard, office-based one. It is worth keeping this in mind next time that you find yourself struggling with the frustrations of the football business.

This isn't to say, of course, that you should be never be dissatisfied with your circumstances and look to improve them: rather, I'm saying keep perspective. Realise that your problems wont last forever. They are merely temporary.

Remember - you are part of a highly competitive industry. It is important to try and stay one step ahead of the game, so try to gain any psychological or physical edge that you can. I needn't remind you of how many people are desperate to make it as a professional footballer. Not only is there a high turnover of home-grown players (you've probably seen many come and go at your own School of Excellence or Academy), but there is also the continually growing influx of foreign players to contend with. You only have to look at the Premier League to realise this: at the time of writing there are 337 foreign players in the Premiership, from 66 different countries. That means that 67% of Premier League footballers are non-British. To become part of the 33% of professionals making a living in the Premier League who are British is a massive challenge – and this is increasingly the case at lower league levels too. But that doesn't mean that it's impossible. Of course it isn't – you just need to maximise every advantage that you can get.

Take your training seriously

It is no surprise that the hardest trainers are normally the best players on match days. It's not rocket science! Remember the Gary Player quote - "the harder I practise the luckier I get." There is simply no substitute for putting in the time and effort on the training pitch.

The well-known author Malcolm Gladwell (writer of The Tipping Point and Outliers) has analysed some of the most successful people in the world. These people come from a wide range of different fields, including sport. In Outliers, a common factor that he identified was the "10,000 hour rule" that we touched on earlier – the theory that one of the keys to success in any field is to practise a specific task for 10,000 hours. This theory has become accepted by many in sporting circles, and adds an element to the nurture v nature debate. Now, obviously, while the quantity of your training is important, the quality is even more crucial – so you should maximise the time that you get to spend in training with skilled coaches. Listen, learn, and practise! practise! practise!

Dr. Solomon Abrahams (PhD, MSc, BSc, MCSP, SRP, OCPPP) is a Clinical Director and Co-Founder of Anatomie Physiotherapy, based in North-West London. He has published over 30 clinical studies in professional medical journals, and has been the physio for one of the top Premier League Football Academies for over 15 years. During this time he has treated international players from England, Denmark, Poland, France and Switzerland (to name just a few). Dr. Abrahams is a massive believer in players taking their training seriously:

"Taking your training seriously is important. Research shows that disciplined regimes tend to the most effective at gaining optimal fitness levels. This includes the physical and mental side of training. This also means having time to rest as well, getting regular sleep and eating well."

I've already mentioned why it is so important to train hard, do extra work and display an attitude of hunger and enthusiasm that sets you apart from the rest of your peers. There are many ways you can do this. Without being a 'suck up,' it can be useful to ask your coach if he can help you do extra work on the elements of your game that he thinks need improving – free kicks, positional sense, first touch, striking a ball with your weaker foot, shooting, etc. – whatever you or your coach feel you need to improve. By spending some one-to-one time with your coaches, they get to know you better as a person, will most probably be willing to help, and will respect the fact that you want to improve. They will appreciate your dedication. There are two obvious benefits to this: you'll score some brownie points, but more importantly, you'll accumulate those 10,000 hours that make you a better player.

Eat well

Get into good eating habits. You don't need to be a slave to your diet, but by the same token, treat your body well – if you consider that food is the fuel that drives your body then you want to give it the best fuel possible, right? You wouldn't put the cheapest, non-purified petrol in a Lamborghini, would you? This is why I would encourage you to steer away from eating fast foods such as McDonalds, Burger King or KFC, and from drinking alcohol in large quantities. Dr. Abrahams concurs:

"Eating well is essential. Having the right food and nutrients maximizes your body's potential. Growing children in particular benefit the most here.

Having protein and vegetables is essential for muscle development. Carbohydrates are also important, to help store energy, but not [by] overdoing it. Certainly, too much fast food - as an example, daily – is not appropriate.

Drinking plenty of fluids daily is also important."

Take some good advice on nutrition from someone who is educated on the topic, especially as everyone's body is different and reacts variably to certain food types. Some players are also prone to putting on weight – Paul Gascoigne was one such player, and he battled with this throughout his career. Stay disciplined and you will soon see and feel the benefits of keeping a healthy balanced diet.

Consider doing pilates and yoga to improve your core strength and flexibility, and stave off injuries

Injuries are an almost inevitable part of being a professional footballer. With daily training (often at high intensity) and regular game time, it is almost impossible to stave off all injuries. There will be times when you pick up a little niggle, or perhaps something worse that will keep you sidelined for a longer period of time. However, you must try to do everything within your own powers to prevent unnecessary injuries occurring. Recent examples demonstrate that regular core strengthening exercises, and those that improve flexibility, help to prevent injuries. Dr. Abrahams testifies to the importance of practising both pilates and yoga as a means to prevent injury:

"Pilates and core strength is essential for a footballer. To create a more dynamic and stronger player, pilates and core stability play a vital role - not only [in] preparing for the physical side of the game, but also in preventing injuries. Also, stretching should be done daily, and not just before and after games."

It might not be the 'coolest' thing to do, but you should consider introducing pilates and yoga into your exercise regime. If you do think it's uncool, bear this in mind: that stigma hasn't stopped a serial medal winner and one of the best players of his generation from claiming yoga as one of the reasons for the length and quality of his illustrious career.

Ryan Giggs's realisation that he needed to start doing something different kicked in when he injured a hamstring in training the day before the Champions League group stage tie v Bayern Munich in November 2001. This injury resulted in him missing a large part of that season.

"It was that day I just thought: 'I need to do something, I need to not drink as much alcohol, I need to look at my diet, I need to do everything I can, my bed, cars – everything to stop this happening.' The hamstring injuries were stopping me probably playing 10 or 15 games a season and I was coming up to 30."

Feeling Good With Yoga: the Secret of Giggs' Success, Ian Herbert, 15th January 2011

At 28 years of age, many people started to write Giggs off, suggesting that he didn't play enough games, and that the hamstring injuries he kept sustaining were thwarting his career. However, with the introduction of yoga into his training regime, he has proved those doubters wrong. He is still putting in first class performances at the very highest level of the game, and at the age of 38!

"Yoga has definitely helped me. It helps me train every day. It gives me the flexibility and strength not only to play the game, but to train as well, and I rarely miss a training session."
Ryan Giggs, Gazzetta dello Sport, 27th March 2012

Don't take your education for granted

A lot of young players feel that they needn't be too bothered about their education, as they won't need it when they become professional footballers. I know how boring it sounds when people keep banging on about the importance of studying – I didn't enjoy school myself. I wasn't particularly academic and I hated studying subjects like maths and science, which I found completely boring. It was only later in life that I began to appreciate just how important an education is, because nothing in life is guaranteed. In football, this is even truer. The sad reality is that relatively few players make it to a good enough level to be able to support themselves.

Steve Quashie, Head of Welfare & Education at Queens Park Rangers, recognises the value in young footballers progressing with their education:

"The continual educational development of all players is a crucial part of a youth player's life. In the [QPR] Youth Department we take our commitment to education very seriously, and we aim to create solid working relationships with schools for our Schoolboys and Apprentices. We view the educational element not only as a 'safety net' should the boys not fulfil their football ambitions, but also [as a means] to teach lifestyle skills that will prove valuable throughout their life as a young player."

There is always the very real chance of a promising career being cut short by serious injury (which is why I always insist that all of my clients take out private career-ending insurance cover). While modern medicine has thankfully put an end to the days when a cruciate ligament injury could end a career,

SHOW ME THE MONEY!

there will always be injuries from which players cannot recover, and I'm not just referring to those sustained while playing football. The injury could be the result of a car crash, or another accident outside of training. Without any other qualifications, how will a player who has had a career-ending injury earn decent money for the rest of his life? This is one powerful reason why I always encourage players never to neglect their education.

I know of very few players that have degrees. A few I can name include Matt Lawrence (currently Gillingham FC – degree in American Studies); Iain Dowie (formerly Crystal Palace and Northern Ireland – degree in engineering); Shaka Hislop (formerly West Ham, Newcastle and Trinidad & Tobago – degree in mechanical engineering); and David Wetherall (formerly Leeds and Bradford – degree in Chemistry). But there aren't too many more that I have heard of or met in my fourteen years in this business. Despite this, though, I think it is important that you have something to fall back on in the event that the dream of becoming a high-earning professional footballer doesn't materialise for you. While you still have the rest of your life ahead of you and can do whatever else you choose to pursue as a career, it is much harder to progress – in any field – without the basic qualifications from school and college. With that in mind, you should make sure you work as hard on your studies as you do on your football. If nothing else, it will benefit your attitude and your career: that kind of discipline will stand you in good stead when approaching any challenge in your life.

I know of a few players who have actually managed to study while they've still been playing. At the time of writing, Dean Furman (Oldham Athletic FC) is pursuing a Sports Science degree in Manchester while another client, Lee Mansell (Torquay United FC), is taking a plumbing course in his spare time.. I recall Nicky Forster (when he moved from Reading to Ipswich in 2005) informing me that he was studying to become a qualified electrician in his spare time, a qualification shared by the current England Under-21 Manager, Stuart Pearce. Pearce, who captained Nottingham Forest and England, was an electrician before he signed for Forest, and famously advertised his services in the match day programme!

Back in the day, it used to be that a footballer would typically open up a sports shop or run a pub when they retired from the game. Today it's very different. Mass media coverage – and in particular the Sky TV revolution – has helped generate vast amounts of money and great opportunities within the football business. These days many ex-players are able to remain professionally connected to the game, be it as coaches, physiotherapists, agents, or media presenters and pundits. However, even when you do make it as a professional footballer, I would still strongly recommend that you never give up on your education. You will have many free hours in the day, so there is absolutely no reason why you couldn't study something that interests you, and which could also be useful to you later on in life.

Someone once said to me, "If you're not growing, you're dying." Heed those words of advice: continue to challenge yourself mentally as well as physically.

Manage your income and expenditure

A good agent will educate a young player about the virtues of saving (or at least not spending more than he earns!). He will help the player set up ISA's, current and savings accounts, and direct debit payments for car insurance, mobile phone bills, car loan repayments, etc. A good agent will assist the player with creating a budget plan, and will regularly check that he is adhering to it.

I cannot stress enough how important it is for a player to develop good spending habits as early as possible. I have seen many young players' finances spiral out of control at the very first sight of an improved contract. The thought of new designer clothes, jewellery, perhaps a new and more expensive car – even gambling – can be irresistible temptations for a young man with access to cash. A good agent will advise the player to enjoy his new wage, but to be sensible with it, and never to spend more than he earns. The agent will normally recommend that the player uses an IFA (Independent Financial Advisor) to structure their savings as efficiently as possible.

No matter how much a player may be earning, whether it is £200 per week or £20,000 per week, the principle remains the same – if they spend more than they earn, at the end of the month they have less than nothing left in their account. Trust me, I have seen plenty of footballers who earn more than £20,000 per week that don't have a penny to their names, and who are, in fact, in large amounts of debt. It's the dreaded 'too much month left at the end of the money' scenario. Not the other way around.

Adam Osper is a registered IFA who heads up the Sports Division of London & Capital – a highly respected Wealth Management Company based in London. Adam and his team provide financial advice to a number of leading Premier League footballers and managers. Here, he explains the importance of getting into good financial habits as early on in your career as possible.

"Having worked with sportsmen for a number of years, I feel one of the key things to ensure financial security when they retire is to get into good habits from a young age. No matter what level of earning, if you start off well and get into good habits like you do on the pitch and in training, you will set yourself up well for the future.

The starting point should be to understand what income you have coming in, and what expenses going out. This is important whether you are earning £1,000, £10,000 or £100,000 per week."

Time management

For a young man striving to reach the heady heights of professional football, time is a precious commodity. There is school or college work to complete, and when this is not dominating life, football training is. This is without even factoring in travel time to and from training.

As the player progresses into the realms of professional football, however, he finds that this battle with time evaporates. On the whole, professional footballers are blessed with fantastic incomes, and, crucially, a great deal of spare time in which to enjoy them! Most clubs in the UK train once a day, and sometimes twice, one day per week. Training normally starts at 10am-10.30am and finishes by 12.30pm, after which time the players are generally free to do whatever they choose, unless they have commercial commitments imposed on them by the club. Some go shopping, play computer games, or spend time with their families and friends. Others have been known to run businesses ranging from property investment to race horse breeding.

Unfortunately, there are also those who get into bad habits in their spare time. Gambling and heavy drinking has long been a plague in football, and one that can be incredibly destructive to players' careers and families – and, ultimately, their mental and physical health. The likes of George Best, Paul Gascoigne, Paul Merson and Tony Adams are just a few examples of this.

Discipline is key

To follow the path to success requires a high level of discipline. This comes in a variety of forms – the discipline you need to eat well, train hard (perhaps even when you don't want to), get homework completed, and stay out of trouble when some of your peers may be out drinking and partying. Young professional footballers are required to mature early on in their lives, and to prioritise what is most important to them. As a parent, it is crucial to try to empathise with your son, and to surround him with as much positivity and support as you can. He'll invariably make mistakes; we all do as we grow up. Just be there to help him overcome his challenges, and keep his eyes on his goals when they waver off track.

The current level of public interest in the lives of professional footballers is unprecedented – a national obsession even! You only have to pick up a newspaper to see that. Gone are the days where sport stars could be found only among the back pages. Nowadays sportsmen – and particularly footballers – are splashed all over the papers, from front to back. Likewise, the social media phenomenon spearheaded by Facebook and Twitter has made the world an even smaller place, where direct public interaction with these superstars is possible. Lack of media training and discipline has lead to one or two high profile players posting some controversial comments on these websites. Wayne Rooney, Rio Ferdinand and Joey Barton are just a few examples of players accused of posting comments that have painted them in an unfavourable light.

People often forget that footballers are normal people who, like any of us, have feelings and can get upset by derogatory comments made about them. But getting upset in public is a bad idea. While I'm not suggesting that players become unemotional robots, they do, however, have to remain disciplined and controlled about what they put in the public domain. We live in the age of 'political correctness,' so better to keep your mouth shut than to open it and cause offense. I'm a massive advocate of letting your football do all the talking for you.

Discipline with food can be tough. There's nothing wrong with having the odd treat, but if you are serious about your career, then it is wise to stick to good eating habits. Generally, this consists of having a healthy breakfast, which might include porridge, some fruit and maybe some toast to act as fuel for the morning session ahead. Lunch and dinner might be protein-based, to help restore some of the energy burned off in that morning session. This could be in the form of lean meats, like chicken or turkey breast, or perhaps grilled fish with salad or vegetables. Pasta, rice and potatoes are also key features on the menu at professional clubs, as these are high in carbohydrates and help to provide energy. Too much of any one food source is generally not good for you, though, so make sure that you balance your diet with a healthy amount of protein, carbohydrates and good fats, rich in omega 3.

There will be times that you don't want to do extra – training in the gym, perhaps, or attending to your studies. There will also be times when you've been training or playing in a match, but you still have homework that needs to be handed in tomorrow. While all of your friends are playing on

Championship Manager or Call of Duty or 'poking' each other on Facebook, you must be disciplined enough to recognise that you are different. If you want to make it as a professional footballer then you have to be prepared to make sacrifices and get your priorities straight. So, get that homework done. Play COD later!

I asked Ross Wilson at Watford to identify what, in his experience, were the main reasons for talented players aged 14-16 falling out of the game – especially in those cases where the player initially seemed nailed on to make it as a top level professional footballer. His answer couldn't have been clearer.

"Mentality. Choices - I'm big on that. Lifestyle, and work ethic. A disability to work hard and appreciate what the game demands.

It doesn't matter whether you are 14, 15 or 18. You need to be able to differentiate yourself from your mates. It maybe OK for your mates to live the lifestyle that they choose (and this goes back to my point about 'choices' and making the right ones), but young footballers who are serious about making a career in the game need to acknowledge that they have so much potential to do something in a different sphere from their mates, and can't necessarily conduct themselves in the same manner as their contemporaries."

Nobody is saying it's easy. If it was then more people would play football for a living. If you have the talent, don't let the wrong attitude be your reason for not making it. There'll be times when friends are out partying the night before a game. They'll be having a drink, chatting up girls and generally having a laugh. It will be very tempting to think, "I'll just go along for an hour or two before going home to bed," but peer pressure has gotten the better of all of us at sometime in our lives – you'd risk turning a quiet night into a full-on bender!

While the temptation is great, always ask yourself first – "is doing this going to help or hinder my performance in training or the game?" This simple question will help you make the right choices.

Only you can decide how much you want to make it as a professional player. What you can be sure of, though, is that there are many others of your age who are experiencing exactly the same challenges as you.

What you can also be certain about is that those who dedicate themselves fully to being the best they can be are generally the ones who make it.

SUMMARY

- £ Work hard on your mental as well as your physical development. You'll need that mental toughness to help you overcome the challenging times ahead

- £ Don't take your ability for granted - if you don't channel it properly, your talent will be surpassed by those with a better attitude and work ethic

- £ Always seek to take out insurance against career-ending injury

- £ Take your training seriously and be prepared to ask your coach for extra help and/or one-to-one tuition to improve relevant aspects of your game

- £ Eat and drink sensibly

- £ Incorporate yoga and pilates into your training regime to help prolong your career and prevent injuries

- £ Remain focused and disciplined.

CHAPTER 8
PRAISE AND SUPPORT

> ❝ Flatter me, and I may not believe you. Criticize me, and I may not like you. Ignore me, and I may not forgive you. Encourage me, and I will not forget you. ❞
>
> William Arthur Ward

A good agent earns his stripes

It is important to have a network of people around you, people who offer you excellent advice and support. These people range from family and friends to your agent. The agent should be more than just "Mr. 5% or 10%" (a common perception of agents by many outside of football).

As previously mentioned, as far as football agents go, there are good guys and bad guys. There are those that have their clients' best interests at heart, and there are those who put themselves first. It is easy for an agent to show up to your son's games and be his best mate when he's playing well, other clubs are watching him, and his club value and appreciate him too. However, it is during the harder times – the times when your lad is struggling with form, injury or off the pitch distractions (maybe family issues, or getting caught up in some trouble with the authorities) – that an agent shows his true colours and earns his stripes.

I have a player that I represent today who asked for my help following poor treatment by his previous agent. Let's call this player 'Lav' for the purposes of this story. Lav was released by a top Premier League club when he was a teenager: he had been with that club since the age of nine, and, finally, the club decided they no longer required his services. Lav was only eighteen at the time and his young spirit was severely dampened. He now found himself in the unfamiliar position of being without a club, without any first team experience, and with no contacts at other clubs. Why would he have contacts? After all, he'd been with the same club for nine years. His agent assured him that he would look after him, and find him a new club; but when push came to shove, the agent went missing. Lav left several messages on the agent's voicemail, and sent him numerous texts, but he never received a reply. Now that he was required to work hard for his player, the agent simply didn't want to know. As for the club, they made no effort to help Lav stay in the professional game by helping source another club. Lav was effectively abandoned. Fortunately, I managed to secure a trial opportunity for Lav, and he grasped it with both hands, securing himself a contract.

In my experience, what happened to Lav is sadly too regular an occurrence. Players are often wrongly promised the world if they sign for certain agents, but when the going gets tough, that agent goes missing. Pay heed to the recommendations of players and parents whose agent has helped them through more challenging times: don't rush into signing with agents who have all the top players, simply because they claim to be the best, or because they turn up to a meeting with a current or ex-pro in an attempt to impress you. Find one you trust, who you know will do his best by you.

Having an inflated opinion of your son's ability

Some parents believe that their son is a 'world beater,' the next Stephen Gerrard or Rio Ferdinand, and nobody can tell them otherwise. What I'd say on this matter is that it is great to have a high opinion of your son's ability; but the career of a professional footballer is not always a smooth one with a pot of gold waiting at the end. More often than not, it's a rocky, bumpy ride with many highs and lows, and with so many obstacles to overcome that all the ability in the world may not be enough.

Be realistic about how good your son might be. Listen to and heed the advice of the coaches and managers who have been in this game for long enough to know (most of the time) at what level your son is likely to end up playing. That isn't to say that he shouldn't still strive for excellence; simply that you should be open-minded and level-headed enough to not over-expect, because if you do, this can place a great and unnecessary pressure on your boy.

Pushy parents are a recipe for disaster

We've all seen them on the touchline at youth games, making their presence felt – screaming at the ref in response to the latest injustice, vocally coaching their son, furiously gesticulating. In the main, their intentions are good - they share the same dream as their child, that of their lad becoming a top professional footballer. But perhaps they want it a bit too desperately!

Many such parents are trying to live their own dreams vicariously through their child, and parents like this can not only be a nightmare for their son to deal with, but also for his club. Invariably, these parents reflect poorly on the child. Young players have enough pressure to deal with as it is, in the various forms of study, training and performing in games, without the added burden of 'overly enthusiastic' parents. In my time I have witnessed several gifted players fall out of love with football due to the pressures exerted on them by their parents. Steve Beaglehole at Leicester City recalls such a scenario:

"I know a player that was sick of his dad pressurizing him. At 16 years old he'd had enough. All his old man seemed to be concerned about was his boy making it as a footballer, so to spite his dad, the boy quit. He tried coming back into the game at 18 but it was too late. The window of opportunity had passed him by"

Obviously, parents like these are in the minority. The sad thing, though, is that, like most 'normal' parents, the majority of them mean no harm. They genuinely want their child to make it, but by pushing too hard they achieve the opposite results.

As a parent I'd encourage you to let the coaches and managers do their jobs. Don't interfere by suggesting that your son is better than the lad playing ahead of him, or that your boy is playing out of position. This is for the coach to decide, and he has his reasons for his choices. Perhaps the coach is experimenting because he feels that the player's attributes may be better suited to a different role.

Experimentation like this is often fruitful: Chris Sutton and Paul Warhurst are just two examples of players who started their professional careers in different positions to the ones in which they ended them. Both were central defenders before being moved into centre forward roles due to injury to other players. In both cases, the switch from heart of defence to pillar of attack proved so fruitful that Sutton and Warhurst earned call-ups to the England National team as strikers. Lucas Radebe, the South African international, who is widely regarded as one of the greatest defenders ever to play for Leeds United, spent 18 months of his career playing in goal!

I'm sure that you wouldn't take too kindly to being told how to do your job by a football coach, so, in most instances I'd advise you strongly just to respect the Coach's ability to perform his role, and accept his decisions gracefully. You never know – what may at first seem like a 'potty' selection may turn out to be a masterstroke!

Approaching coaches and managers

There is nothing wrong with asking a coach or manager questions about his decisions, or how about they think your son is developing, but be careful with how you approach the subject. Tact and discretion are the order of the day: the last thing a coach wants is to feel undermined. Be polite and friendly, and I'm sure you'll get the same in return.

Coaches have many players to deal with, so they're very busy people – if you would like to have a chat about your son, it is best to schedule a meeting formally. Don't approach the coach during or straight after a game, when their thoughts are elsewhere and their emotions are often riding high. A mutually convenient time, in private, outside of training hours, will be a much better space in which to communicate. You'll find that your questions will be better received, and answered in a more relaxed environment.

A good agent makes themselves redundant

My role as agent is not simply about being at the beck and call of my clients. Sure – at times I am happy to assist them with entry to clubs, concerts and other social events, but primarily I view my role as being a support system. In essence, my job is to ensure that my players have nothing to worry about off the pitch, so that they can fully focus on their actions on it. However – and this will probably surprise you – my ultimate goal is to eventually make myself redundant to my clients.

That may sound crazy, but let me explain what I mean.

Is doing everything with the exception of playing and training for a player the definition of a good service, or does it actually harm his development as a human being?

I consider the answer to be the latter. It harms his development as a human being.

Why? Because when it comes to the time in his life when I am no longer around, who will run his life for him? Who will look after his bank accounts, investments, holiday plans, car and property purchases and so on? Who will complete all the other tasks that are part of being a responsible adult?

For this reason, I aim to help my clients bring some order and stability into their lives, while empowering them to make their own decisions. Ultimately, I want to leave them with the tools to control their own lives.

Lao Tzu put it perfectly when he said:

"Give a man a fish, he'll eat for a day. Teach a man to fish and he'll eat for a lifetime."

Lao Tzu, the Chinese Founder of Taoism, 4th Century BC

If a player isn't taught how to 'fish', he can become overly dependent. There can be disastrous consequences when an agent 'mothers' his clients excessively. Some agents will even take complete control of their clients' bank accounts – and for some, sadly, the temptation is too great. After years have past, accusations of theft are not uncommon. In early 2011, the FA-Licensed agent Ian Elliott was publicly accused of precisely this by England international winger Stewart Downing. The case went to court, where Downing accused Elliott of having siphoned more than £500,000 from his bank account.

It is an agent's responsibility to educate his player always to be courteous and respectful when communicating with coaches. There are times when it's appropriate for an agent to step in and talk on his player's behalf, but in the main it is healthier for a player to use his own voice – especially in football matters. Direct communication offers less scope for misunderstanding, and more scope for agreement. Perhaps even more importantly, it provides an opportunity for the player to demonstrate maturity and develop as a responsible adult. Going to speak with the Manager is often the most difficult task a young player can do, as they are fearful of a negative reaction. However, such directness shows great personal strength – something that will be respected by any decent manager, when delivered respectfully. If an agent or guardian asks the same questions on the player's behalf, then the opportunity to demonstrate character is lost.

The 3 'R's for building rapport - Respect, Respect, Respect

The old adage says "respect has to be earned"; but I adopt a very different philosophy.

I believe, strongly, that respect should be there to begin with, and is only ever lost, not gained. Apart from being the right thing to do, if you treat someone with respect from the outset, you will probably be treated equally well in return. This doesn't only apply to respecting your elders (senior professional players, coaches, managers and administration staff at the club), but it extends to your team-mates too. When a dressing room is full of individuals who respect each other, the true definition of the word 'team' is in effect. It's no coincidence that the word 'team' has often been used as an acronym for Together Everyone Achieves More.

This principle has never been better exemplified than in 1988, when Wimbledon's 'Crazy Gang' achieved the unimaginable by defeating the mighty Liverpool in the FA Cup Final. Liverpool were so dominant in the First Division (as it was then) that they had won the League title in nine of the previous 13 seasons. During that period they had also accumulated four League Cups, one FA Cup and – most impressively – four European Cups. In contrast, making the story even more of a fairy tale, only five seasons earlier Wimbledon had been playing in the old Fourth Division! Their success that day at Wembley was built on solid teamwork and respect for each other. So was their magnificent achievement of maintaining top-flight football for fourteen years. In that team, the players played their hearts out for each other, and for a succession of 'big personality' managers - originally Dave Bassett, then Bobby Gould, Ray Harford, and Joe Kinnear. The group was the essence of synergy - the idea that a cohesive group is more than the sum of its parts.

There are many different ways to build rapport and respect with team-mates. A hard working training atmosphere and some opportunities to share social experiences together outside of the football environment are a good place to start. Maybe going for lunch together, or doing something fun, like go-karting or paintballing. Spending some free time together as a team will help you get to know one another better and develop unity. This 'closeness' often relays itself onto the pitch and shows up in improved team performances and results. A positive relationship off the pitch normally translates to a positive one on it.

Of course, there have been exceptions to this rule. You might never have known it, but Teddy Sheringham and Andy Cole, who formed such a potent strike partnership at Manchester United, were anything but friends off the pitch. When on it, however, they seemed to have an almost telepathic understanding that resulted in some outstanding performances. This is a rare situation though. Here were two exceptional players, who perhaps didn't respect one another as people; but there could be no question that they respected each other's ability as footballers – and the results speak for themselves.

While it is important for players to be able to have a laugh and a joke with their team-mates, they must also respect boundaries. Cross the line by making an offensive comment about a team mate's religion, cultural beliefs, family, or partner, and the damage to a player-to-player relationship can be irreparable.

It goes without saying that the ethos of respect extends to the coaching staff, too: keeping his coaches on his side is crucial to your son's progress.

Positivity

"No one can make you feel inferior without your consent."
Eleanor Roosevelt

For me, this brilliant quote points to the secret to staying positive: ultimately, being confident and optimistic is a choice. That said, though, remaining positive can be tough for a player who is enduring a dip in performance, or recovering from an injury. Footballers everywhere will sometimes get knocked down by criticism, but it is up to them not to allow others to make them feel incapable of succeeding. Even if a player is consistently told that he's the best in the world, if he doesn't have the self-belief he quite simply won't make it.

A client of mine, Dean Furman, today admits that there were times when he was a schoolboy at Chelsea, that he felt slightly inferior to other players. He almost didn't believe that he was good enough to be playing with some of the other lads, especially those a bit older than him who were involved with England Under-16s or Under-17s. This negative perception of himself would occasionally be reflected in his performances – a fear of making mistakes would creep in that would stop him from expressing the full range of his skills. This was all, of course, self-destructive internal chat that quite simply wasn't true. The truth was something very different: Dean was more than good enough to play in that team. Thankfully, after 6 months of training full-time with the likes of Jack Cork, Michael Mansienne, Scott Sinclair, Ryan Bertrand and Liam Bridcutt (all of whom are now playing at a good professional level) and cementing his position in the team, his self-confidence blossomed. Furman (see picture section) went on to excel at Glasgow Rangers, where he captained the Youth Team to a Cup and League double during the 2006-07 season, earning himself an improved contract in the process.

While praise and progression can certainly help to foster a positive attitude, there will be times when a player doubts himself nonetheless. At these difficult times, he must draw upon his previous experiences, remembering when he felt confident in his ability, and recognising that if he wasn't good enough, he wouldn't be where he is.

Another thing that helps is the decision to adopt an 'attitude of gratitude!' I cannot imagine a better job than being a top-class footballer. A young pro should be grateful for his talent and the opportunity to pursue something that he is passionate about, and which can earn him some fantastic money. Most football agents are frustrated footballers who would much rather be putting on the boots and sharing the banter in the dressing room than picking up the mobile phones trying to broker deals. There can be nothing like the buzz of pulling on the first team or international team shirt and running out to the cheers of tens of thousands of fans singing your name in admiration.

If I could only make just one single point to a young player striving to become a top level professional footballer, it would be this: it is you that will get yourself to where you ultimately end up. Nobody else.

For parents: your son's future is firmly in his own hands. There may be times when he'd like to relinquish that responsibility, but ultimately that is the truth of the matter. Nobody else can put in the work on the training pitch or play for him in the games. Yes, there will be times when he'll need a bit of luck – a coach taking a shine to him, an agent using his contacts to find him a new club if he is released. But 'luck' plays a far less significant role in the pursuit of success than the ability, attitude and focus of the player himself.

The 'attitude of gratitude' ethos should also extend to the way in which a young player treats his parents and his supporters. Sadly, I have seen far too many players take these things for granted. Many parents invest a lot of time in driving their sons to training and games, and often have to take time off from work to do so. The responsibility for being on time, making sure their son eats right and gets enough sleep, and providing support through the good and the bad times sits pretty firmly on their shoulders as their son grows up as a player. I'm sure that there are plenty of other things parents could be doing with their days instead of chaperoning their kids. Players: thank these people for their time, effort and encouragement.

Supportive parents

The support of his parents is crucial to an aspiring young player's chances of making it as a professional footballer. A career as a player will contain times of self-doubt, frustration and disappointment where a young man would be lost without the love and backing of his family.

Sometimes, a young player may be lucky enough to experience rapid success, but this, too, has its pitfalls. Under these circumstances, a player may need to be monitored and 'tamed' slightly, in order to keep his feet firmly on the ground and avoid his developing an "I've already made it" attitude.

Feeling as though we are loved and supported helps us to build self-confidence and belief in ourselves. I have no doubt that far more successful players come from strong loving families than those that don't. We learn a great deal in the early stages of our lives from our parents, and tend to adopt their traits and behaviours: most of us are conditioned from an early age by being told what is good and what is bad, and what we can and can't do. This is how our values and beliefs are formed. By the same token, the encouragement, praise and guidance we receive while we grow up is fundamental to the way we see ourselves, and our ability to be successful.

In my time as an agent I have seen both the pushy parents who have driven their sons away from the game, and the gently supportive ones who have helped their boys to achieve their best, without killing their love of football. One of the most rewarding moments in my career so far was not making good commission on a big money transfer, but rather the day I was present at Adam Lallana's debut game for England Under-18s v Slovenia. The great joy I felt was due to the fact that I had grown to view Adam as a good friend as well as a valued client. I had also become close to his family, and I very much shared the great pride they felt that day.

Adam and I always spoke regularly, and I attended as many of his games that I could. I shared in the times of his frustration with his struggle to find first team football, despite his talent and ability to play top level football being so obvious to me. However, through adversity can blossom real strength of character, and, as his subsequent career path proves, Adam has that in abundance – he is now regarded as one of the best players outside of the Premier League.

On that day when he turned out for England, the fact that so many of Adam's family members and friends were there to witness him representing his country, in his home town of Bournemouth, made the whole occasion extra special. My point here is that Adam's success to date has, in large part, been due to his upbringing and to the support that his family and friends have given him over the years. I have no doubt that he'll continue to excel in the Premiership with newly-promoted Southampton. He doesn't just have the ability and work ethic: he also possesses that 'attitude of gratitude' for the many blessings that he has in his life. Good luck to him.

So: taking your boy to training, being at games to cheer him on, and building rapport with coaches and other players' parents are all very important to your son's progress. I understand how easy it can be to get caught up in the emotion of a game in which your child is playing, but it is crucial to maintain a clear perspective and recognise that every game and training session is geared towards his development. This does not necessarily mean that he has to win every time he plays. Whatever you do, please steer clear of trying to coach your child from the sidelines – this is something upon which coaches do not look favourably!

Try to steer clear from criticising your son's game at all, in fact, regardless of how constructive you think you're being. This is firstly because the suggestions you make may conflict with those of his coaches, which can lead to confusion. You will probably have your own views, but I think it is best to leave the coaching to the coaches! Secondly, and perhaps more importantly, the criticism of a parent can cut deep. Football is a game that is best played when a player is confident enough to express himself. The praise and encouragement of a parent can be instrumental to a young man's ability to do this.

When you think about it, your son is probably under more pressure than most lads his age. He has his school or college workload to contend with as well as his training schedule. We all know that it is common for many boys aged 14-18 to rebel against their parents' wishes, but if this happens, it is still crucial to let them know that you are there to listen, and to be a support mechanism. Sometimes what a young players needs is not feedback or advice, but rather the ear and shoulder of someone they can trust.

On some occasions, though, this support role can be an inappropriate one for a parent to play – it is normal for a young man to want to keep certain aspects of his life private. In these instances, a good agent can be the ideal person in whom to confide – a wise old head, perhaps, but also a mate.

Building rapport with agents and clubs

Some clubs will advise players and their families against having an agent representing them when they are young. This is generally done in an attempt to prevent bad agents from getting their claws into young pros. A bad agent will typically try to move a player to another club for his own financial gain, with little regard for the player's development, and protecting young players from these bad agents is an understandable and justified concern for a club to have. It can also be incredibly frustrating for a Youth Team Manager when they have built a strong team only for a key player to be enticed away, as this can potentially break up the dynamic of the team.

The job of an agent is to look after the best interests of his player, whereas the job of a Youth Team Manager is to develop and nurture young talent. In the right circumstances, where both parties are doing a good job, the two co-exist effectively, as their primary concern should not be dissimilar – the welfare of the player. If that player is moved on, then it is only because the Youth Manager and his coaching staff have done a very good job with developing the player, and so the move should be financially straightforward and logical. In the 'football world,' however, where we are dealing with people and emotions and not products, logic can be a commodity that is hard to come by.

It is important for young players and parents to respect the opinion of the club, but at the same time not to be bullied by them, and to understand that, ultimately, it is the player's choice whether to sign with an agent or not. Many clubs believe that a player doesn't need an agent prior to signing their first professional contract. Their argument is: "what purpose does an agent serve at that stage in a player's career, other than to distract him from his football with financial matters?"

Generally speaking, this is a pretty fair question – but not in every instance. Each situation must be taken on its individual merits. For example, if a player is not offered a scholarship, what is the most effective way for him to find another club? The answer is surely, "by using an agent."

I'm not suggesting that a 16-year-old footballer should have an agent as a matter of course. Unless he wants someone who can get him free boots, or get him into nightclubs, he may not need one. As a parent, though, I would recommend that you initially familiarise yourself with a few agents, in order to get to know what they are about, and what they can offer. You'll be able to compare and contrast what they have to say and gauge which one(s) you feel most comfortable with. Once you have done this I would then suggest only staying in touch with one or two that you like to avoid confusion and mixed opinions while getting to know them better. That way, when it does become appropriate to use an agent. you will have the correct match for your son already lined up.

For the record, I don't believe that a player should sign with an agent just because he may be able to get him some free boots and access to nightclubs! When these distractions make an appearance, always think back to the basic principles, the basic questions: does the player want someone who is going to help him achieve his football career goals, or would he rather have an agent who bribes him with freebies and the opportunity to be distracted from playing football?!

Negativity is all around us

This section is for your son...

Have you ever experienced a time in your life when you felt fantastic and unstoppable? You felt so certain that in that moment you just knew you couldn't possibly fail at whatever you set your mind to?

My next question is, how many times have you enjoyed that same, invincible feeling in your life? I would like to wager a bet that your answer is far less than the number of times when you have felt down on your luck, miserable, with a sense of failure and other negative emotions.

This is because most of us are conditioned to think negatively, to expect the worst and to avoid any kind of physical or emotional pain. This means that we rarely step out of our comfort zones.

Negativity is all around us. From a young age we aren't told as much what we can do, as what we can't. You may have heard some of these comments before: "you can't make it as a footballer, you aren't... big enough, good enough, mentally strong enough, can't use your left foot, haven't got the discipline, etc." If you were to listen to such comments, you wouldn't even bother carrying on.

The road to success is full of obstacles. One of those is dealing with the negative energy you create in your own self. Another is dealing with the negativity that comes from external sources.

There may be some people who you consider your friends, but who are actually a negative influence on your life. They may try to lead you astray, coercing you into clubbing, partying and drinking at times that are totally inappropriate, or simply illegal if you are under age. This is often born out of simple jealousy. This is one good reason to pick your friends very carefully. I know of a League One player who is lucky enough to have some very supportive friends, but he also has a couple who are clearly a bit envious of his career. These 'friends' are disparaging of the level that he plays at, and take no interest in supporting him at games. Funny, because I'd wager that they'd swap jobs with him in a heartbeat.

Peter Horne at Bradford City told me about a talented young player who unfortunately developed a poor attitude as a result of spending time with people that were a bad influence on him.

"We once had a lad that scored 60-70 goals in a season who just went off the rails, and it just got too bad and it was affecting our players here. And you can't risk that, no matter how talented a lad might be. It was a change in character that I've never seen happen so quickly before, and I've no doubt it was as a result of the people he was hanging around with outside of football. It developed over the space of a year. His persona changed completely. From being a very polite and friendly young lad and great kid, it all changed. Clearly, we couldn't risk keeping him on board. He wasn't valuable enough to us for us to let him ruin the bunch of players we had here. No lad is bigger or more valuable than the club or group."

It isn't just friends who can fuel the negativity, either. Sometimes family members are guilty of that too. I remember a player whose brother was once a promising young footballer, but who lost his way and spent the subsequent years reminding anyone who would hear of it how talented he was - more than his brother, according to him! The saying, 'the older I get, the better I was' springs to mind. This behaviour was nothing more than thinly-veiled bitterness, and his unwillingness to support his younger brother with his own footballing ambitions couldn't have been clearer. You can't pick your family, of course, but the lesson to learn from these examples is to be careful from whom you take advice, and with whom you decide to spend most of your time. As the famous American entrepreneur and motivational speaker Jim Rohn said: "you are the average of the five people you spend the most time with." If this is true, then you might want to think about who those five people are, and whether they have a negative or positive effect on your life.

SUMMARY

FOR PARENTS

- £ Get to know a few reputable agents. You never know when you may need to call on their expertise. Narrow these down to one or two to stay in regular contact with.
- £ Encourage, support and praise your son. Try to avoid criticism of his game or his coaches.
- £ Let the coaching staff do their jobs and avoid being labelled a 'pushy parent'. Clubs hate them!
- £ Be courteous and friendly to club staff. Do this, and you should receive the same in return.

FOR PLAYERS

- £ It is very important that you build a strong rapport with your team-mates, coaching staff and agent
- £ It is vital to remain mentally positive: there will be many challenges to overcome in the years ahead
- £ Make sure you choose your friends wisely
- £ With supportive family and friends, you have a far greater chance of succeeding in your career.

APPENDIX
Standard Football Association Representation Agreement between a licensed agent and a player

Below is a standard FA representation contract between an FA Licensed agent and a player. I would like to extend my thanks to the English Football Association for allowing me to illustrate this document. It must also be noted, however, that this document was taken at the time of writing (2011-12 season) and is subject to change in the future.

REPRESENTATION CONTRACT between AGENT and PLAYER

THIS REPRESENTATION CONTRACT is made the   day of
BETWEEN [NAME OF INDIVIDUAL AUTHORISED AGENT] (the 'Authorised Agent') [LICENCE / REGISTRATION NUMBER] of [COMPANY NAME and ADDRESS (where applicable)] (the 'Company') and [THE PLAYER] [ADDRESS] [D.O.B.] (the 'Player')

WHEREAS

(1) The Authorised Agent has informed the Player in writing that he should consider taking independent legal advice in relation to this Representation Contract and he has afforded the Player the opportunity to take such legal advice prior to the execution of this Representation Contract.
(2) The Player has provided written confirmation in the form set out at Appendix 1 to this Representation Contract on or before the date of this Representation Contract that either (i) he has obtained such legal advice or (ii) he has decided that he does not need to do so.

IT IS HEREBY AGREED as follows:

APPOINTMENT

1. The Player hereby appoints the Authorised Agent to provide services on the following terms:
[describe the detail and nature of the services].
[The Player is contracted to the Authorised Agent on an exclusive basis in accordance with clause 3 below]
or [delete as applicable]
[The Player is contracted to the Authorised Agent on a non-exclusive basis in accordance with clause 5 below].

(the 'Services')

TERM

2. The term of this Representation Contract shall, subject to clauses 13 to 16 below, be for a period of [MONTHS/YEARS up to a maximum of 2 years] from the date hereof at the end of which it shall terminate without notice. The Representation Contract may be renewed at any time upon the written agreement of both parties, provided that the term of the Representation Contract renewed by the parties shall not be for a term of more than 2 years.

NATURE OF THE RELATIONSHIP

3. [IF AGREEMENT IS EXCLUSIVE UNDER CLAUSE 1 - For the term of this Representation Contract the Player shall engage no other Authorised Agent (as defined in The Football Association Football Agents Regulations (the 'Agents Regulations') in relation to, or to provide, the Services without the written consent of the Authorised Agent.]

4. [IF AGREEMENT IS NON-EXCLUSIVE UNDER CLAUSE 1- Where the Authorised Agent has not performed any Services for the Player in respect of any particular Transaction or Contract Negotiation (as defined in the Agents Regulations) pursuant to the terms of this Representation Contract, no payment shall be due or payable to the Authorised Agent in respect of such Transaction or Contract Negotiation under the terms hereof.]

5. [IF AGREEMENT IS NON-EXCLUSIVE UNDER CLAUSE 1- The Player shall be entitled to appoint any other authorised agents (as defined in the Agents Regulations) to provide the Services during the term of this Representation Contract.]

6. The Player shall not be obliged to use the services of the Authorised Agent during the term of this Representation Contract and may represent himself in any Transaction or Contract Negotiation (as defined in the Agents Regulations) should he so desire.

REMUNERATION

7. In consideration for the provision of the Services, the Player shall pay to the Authorised Agent a fee in accordance with the requirements of the Agents Regulations and the terms of this Representation Contract as follows:
[Set out full details of the fee payable both during the Representation Contract and after expiry of the Representation Contract (e.g. an hourly rate, a percentage of earnings by periodic instalments, post-termination entitlement etc) and specify the terms upon which it is payable, (e.g. 30 days after receipt of invoice) and the regularity of payment (e.g. at the commencement of the playing contract, monthly/quarterly/annual instalments]
The above sums being exclusive of any Value Added Tax that may be payable.

8. Payment of the sums due above shall be made subject to receipt by the Player of the Authorised Agent's written invoices therefor.

9. The Authorised Agent shall bear all expenses incurred in performing his duties under this Representation Contract and the Player shall not be liable to make any payments not expressly set out herein.

OBLIGATIONS

10. The Authorised Agent undertakes and warrants to the Player that he will at all times during the term of this Representation Contract perform the Services conscientiously and in the best interests of the Player and, in particular:
a. he shall provide the Services to the best of his ability and use all reasonable endeavours in connection therewith;
b. he shall keep the Player informed of any and all material information

relating to the provision of the Services and shall not enter into negotiations with any third parties on the Player's behalf without the Player's consent;
c. he shall comply with the Rules of the Football Association and the Agents Regulations;
d. he holds, and will continue to hold, a current valid licence/registration issued by The Football Association;
e. he has, and shall maintain, in place valid and effective professional liability insurance in respect of the Services and shall, at the Player's request, provide the Player with a copy of the policy;
f. he shall not, either directly or indirectly, make payments of any kind to, or receive payments of any kind from, a Club (as defined in the Agents Regulations), which results from the provision of the Services, save where permitted in accordance with the Agents Regulations;
g. he shall not incur any liability in excess of £1000 on behalf of the Player without the prior consent of the Player;
h. he shall, on or before 30 November each year, provide an itemised statement (in the form prescribed by The Football Association from time to time) to the Player covering the period from 1 October of the previous year to 30 September of the relevant year, which sets out any and all remuneration or payments of whatever nature, including in relation to Commercial Rights (as defined in the Agents Regulations), charged by the Authorised Agent to the Player during that period.

11. The Player undertakes and warrants to the Authorised Agent that:
a. he is free to enter into the Representation Contract and is not prevented or restricted from so doing by any other extant agreement with another authorised agent or otherwise;
b. [IF AGREEMENT IS EXCLUSIVE UNDER CLAUSE 1 - he shall notify the Authorised Agent of any approach or offer or inquiry that the Player receives from any other authorised agent, club or person acting directly or indirectly on behalf of a club that falls within the scope of the Services. The Player shall not be entitled to engage the services of another authorised agent without the prior written consent of the Authorised Agent;]
c. he shall comply with the Rules of the Football Association and the Agents Regulations;
d. he shall provide any such information that the Authorised Agent may reasonably require in order to enable the Authorised Agent to perform the Services hereunder; and
e. where permitted by this Representation Contract, if he makes a written

request to a club that the club deal with someone other than the Authorised Agent, including with the Player himself, in relation to a Transaction or Contract Negotiation (as defined within the Agents Regulations) he shall provide the Authorised Agent with a copy of the written request as soon as reasonably practical and in any event within 5 days of its execution.

PLAYER CONSENT

12 Unless and until otherwise advised by the Player to the Authorised Agent in writing, the Player consents to the Authorised Agent providing services in respect of the Player to any Club to which the Player may become contracted (or with which he may renew a playing contract) during the term of this agreement provided always that the requirements relating to Player Consent as set out in the Agents Regulations are complied with in full, and provided that the provision of such services shall not be to the detriment of the Authorised Agent's primary responsibility to represent the Player honestly and efficiently pursuant to his obligations under this Representation Contract.

TERMINATION

13. If the Authorised Agent's licence/registration is suspended or withdrawn during the term of this Representation Contract as determined by The Football Association or other relevant national association or FIFA, and the relevant appeal process has been exhausted where applicable, then this Representation Contract shall be automatically terminated with immediate effect.

14. If either party:
a. commits a material breach of this Representation Contract which is not capable of remedy;
b. commits a material breach of this Representation Contract which is capable of being remedied but fails to remedy such breach within 30 days of a receipt of written notice from the non-defaulting party specifying the breach and requiring it to be remedied; or
c. is declared bankrupt [or, in the case of the Authorised Agent only, if the Company becomes insolvent], this Representation Contract may be terminated by the non-defaulting party on written notice with immediate effect.

15. Any sums that fall due for payment to the Authorised Agent after termination of this Representation Contract, other than those sums arising out of rights that have been accrued before termination, shall not be due and payable by the Player if:
a. the Representation Contract is terminated in accordance with clause 13; or
b. the Representation Contract is terminated in accordance with clause 14 to the extent only that the material breach giving rise to such termination is committed by the Authorised Agent

16. [WHERE THE AUTHORISED AGENT IS EMPLOYED OR RETAINED ON BEHALF OF AN ORGANISATION - Should the Authorised Agent, during the term of this Representation Contract, cease to be an employee or director or other authorised representative of the Company, the Player shall be informed in writing by the Authorised Agent as soon as reasonably practicable thereafter, and the Player shall be given the option to:
a. continue to be represented by the Authorised Agent under this Representation Contract subject to any provisions, restrictions or obligations that may exist between the Authorised Agent and the Company; or
b. terminate the Representation Contract and be represented by, and enter into a representation contract with, another authorised agent employed by the Company without any further obligations to the Authorised Agent other than in respect of any outstanding sums that are or shall be due to the Authorised Agent hereunder (subject to the relevant provisions of the Agents Regulations regarding entitlement to remuneration and to any provisions or obligations that may exist between the Authorised Agent and the Company); or
c. terminate the Representation Contract and, if he so wishes, seek alternative representation without any further obligations to the Authorised Agent and/or the Company other than in respect of any outstanding sums that are or shall be due to the Authorised Agent hereunder (subject to the relevant provisions of the Agents Regulations regarding entitlement to remuneration and any provisions or obligations that may exist between the Authorised Agent and the Company).
[The Player shall be required to notify the Authorised Agent in writing of his election within 28 days of receiving notice from the Authorised Agent of his change in circumstances, and in the event that the Player elects the option set out in clause 16(b) above, the Authorised Agent shall sign any documents and do any acts as may be necessary to novate this Representation Contract to a third party authorised agent employed by the Company.]

NOTICES

17. All notices to be given under this Representation Contract shall be in writing in English and left at or sent by first class registered or recorded delivery mail or facsimile to the address of the party as set out above or to such other address and/or addresses as the party concerned shall from time to time designate by written notice pursuant hereto.

18. Any such notice shall be deemed given, in the case of hand delivery, at the time when the same is left at the addressee's address or, in the case of first class registered post or recorded delivery mail, on the business day after delivery or, in the case of a facsimile, upon transmission by the sender provided that the transmitting facsimile machine generates upon completion of the transmission a transmission report stating that the notice has been duly transmitted without error to the addressee's facsimile number.

SEVERABILITY

19. If any term or provision in this Representation Contract shall be held to be illegal, invalid or unenforceable, in whole or part, under any enactment or rule of law, such term or provision or part shall to that extent be deemed not to form part of this Representation Contract but the legality, validity and enforceability of the remainder of this Representation Contract shall not be affected.

CONFIDENTIALITY

20. Save as required by law or any fiscal or regulatory authority (including The Football Association), each party undertakes [to keep the terms of this Representation Contract and any information of a confidential nature that he may receive in respect of the other party during the term of this Representation Contract strictly confidential and shall at no time (whether before or after expiry of the term of this Representation Contract) divulge any such information to any third party (other than to their respective professional advisors) without the consent of the other party.]

ENTIRE AGREEMENT

21. This Representation Contract sets out the entire agreement between the parties hereto, in relation to those matters set out herein, and supersedes all prior discussions statements representations and undertakings between them or their advisors.

22. Clause 21 shall not exclude any liability which either party would otherwise have to the other or any right which either of them may have to rescind this Representation Contract in respect of any statements made fraudulently by the other prior to the execution of this Representation Contract or any rights which either of them may have in respect of fraudulent concealment by the other.

23. This Representation Contract may not be amended, modified or superseded unless expressly agreed to in writing by both parties.

RELATIONSHIP BETWEEN THE PARTIES

24. The Authorised Agent is not authorised under this Representation Contract to enter into employment contracts on behalf of the Player or bind the Player in a contractual relationship in any way whatsoever, [save as provided for under Clause 10(g)].

SURVIVAL OF RIGHTS, DUTIES AND OBLIGATIONS

25. Expiry or termination of this Representation Contract shall not release the parties from any liability or right of action or claim which at the time of such expiry or termination has already accrued or may accrue to either party in respect of any act or omission prior to such expiry or termination.
26. Expiry or termination shall not affect the coming into force or the continuance in force of any provision hereof which is expressly or by implication intended to come into or continue in force on or after such termination.

NON-ASSIGNMENT

27. The Authorised Agent shall not assign, subcontract or novate the benefit or burden of this Representation Contract or of any of its provisions

without the prior consent in writing of the Player (such consent to be given or withheld in the Player's absolute discretion) and in any case shall not assign, subcontract or novate the benefit or burden of this Representation Contract or of any of its provisions to an Unauthorised Agent (as defined in the Agents Regulations).

THIRD PARTY RIGHTS

28. Notwithstanding any other provision of this Representation Contract, a person who is not a party to this Representation Contract has no rights under the Contracts (Rights of Third Parties) Act 1999 to rely upon or enforce any term of this Representation Contract.

SUPPLEMENTAL AGREEMENTS

29. Any other arrangements between the parties in any way connected to the provision of the Services that are supplemental to this Representation Contract shall be in accordance with the requirements of the Agents' Regulations and shall be annexed to the Representation Contract and submitted to The Football Association (and other relevant national association) for registration together with this Representation Contract.

DISPUTES

30. Any dispute between the parties arising from this Representation Contract which constitutes a breach of the Rules of the Football Association and/or the Agents Regulations shall be dealt with by the Rules of the Football Association in the first instance and referred to FIFA where appropriate. Any other dispute between the parties shall be dealt with as between the parties under Rule K (Arbitration) of the Rules of the Football Association (as may vary from time to time).

GOVERNING LAW & JURISDICTION

31. This Representation Contract shall be governed by and construed and interpreted in accordance with the laws of England and Wales and, subject to clause 30 above, the parties hereby submit to the exclusive jurisdiction of the courts of England and Wales.

SIGNATURES

This contract has been signed in fourfold and the copies have been distributed to:
i. The National Association with which the Authorised Agent is registered
ii. The National Association with which the Player is registered (if different)
iii. The Authorised Agent
iv. The Player

Signed by the Player: _____
Date: _____

(and Guardian if the Player is a minor)

Print Name: _____
Signed by the Guardian: _____
Date: _____

(if the Player is a minor)

Print Name: _____

Signed by the Authorised Agent: _____
Date: _____

LODGEMENT

The Football Association: _____
Date: _____

Other National Association: _____
Date: _____

APPENDIX 1: Independent Legal Advice Confirmation

I [insert player's name] confirm that I received independent legal advice from [Lawyer's name] of [name of firm] as to the terms and effect of this Representation Contract.
OR
I [insert player's name] confirm that I have been advised by [insert authorised agent's name] to consider taking independent legal advice in relation to the terms of this Representation Contract, and that I have been given a reasonable opportunity to take such independent legal advice, but that I have decided that I do not need to do so.

Signed by the Player: _____
Date: _____

(and Guardian if the Player is a minor)

Print Name: _____
Signed by the Guardian: _____
Date: _____

(if the Player is a minor)

Print Name: _____

Printed in Great Britain
by Amazon.co.uk, Ltd.,
Marston Gate.